Common Evil

Common Evil

Political Economy *and* the Ethics of Liberation

Andrew T. Vink

ORBIS BOOKS
Maryknoll, New York 10545

Founded in 1970, Orbis Books endeavors to publish works that enlighten the mind, nourish the spirit, and challenge the conscience. The publishing arm of the Maryknoll Fathers and Brothers, Orbis seeks to explore the global dimensions of the Christian faith and mission, to invite dialogue with diverse cultures and religious traditions, and to serve the cause of reconciliation and peace. The books published reflect the views of their authors and do not represent the official position of the Maryknoll Society. To learn more about Maryknoll and Orbis Books, please visit our website at www.orbisbooks.com.

Copyright © 2025 by Andrew T. Vink

Published by Orbis Books, Box 302, Maryknoll, NY 10545-0302.

All rights reserved.

No part of this publication may be reproduced or transmitted in any form or by any means, electronic or mechanical, including photocopying, recording, or any information storage or retrieval system, without prior permission in writing from the publisher.

Queries regarding rights and permissions should be addressed to: Orbis Books, P.O. Box 302, Maryknoll, NY 10545-0302.

Manufactured in the United States of America

Library of Congress Cataloging-in-Publication Data

Names: Vink, Andrew T. author
Title: Common evil : political economy and the ethics of liberation / Andrew T. Vink.
Description: Maryknoll, NY : Orbis Books, [2025] | Includes bibliographical references and index. | Summary: "Christian theology for the common good that critiques the common evil found in economic exploitation and injustice"—Provided by publisher.
Identifiers: LCCN 2025026267 (print) | LCCN 2025026268 (ebook) | ISBN 9781626986411 trade paperback | ISBN 9798888660966 epub
Subjects: LCSH: Economics—Religious aspects—Christianity | Common good—Religious aspects—Christianity | Political theology
Classification: LCC BR115.E3 V56 2025 (print) | LCC BR115.E3 (ebook) | DDC 261.8/5—dc23/eng/20250620
LC record available at https://lccn.loc.gov/2025026267
LC ebook record available at https://lccn.loc.gov/2025026268

To Elisabeth

Contents

Acknowledgments ix

Prelude: A Missing Hope xi
   Ideoligization xvi
   Historicization xix
   The Journey Ahead xxi

1. The Common Evil 1
   Articulating the Common Good 2
   Articulating the Common Evil 12
   The Common Evil as Integral Dehumanization 24
   Conclusion 39

2. Obstructing the Reign of God: Soteriological Implications 41
   Understanding the Reign of God: Salvation of and in History 42
   Obstructing the Reign of God: The Common Evil in Action 56
   Working toward the Reign of God: Defining a Humanizing Praxis 70
   Conclusion 79

3. A Political Theology of Dissent: Politico-Economic Impacts — 81
The Civilizations of Wealth and Poverty — 82
The Economic Question of Unemployment — 103
The Political Theology of Dissent — 108
Articulating the Dissent: Three Primary Directives — 113

4. Identifying the Obstruction: Neoliberalism as the Common Evil — 121
Identifying the Injustice — 122
Jung Mo Sung and Desire, Market, Religion — 125
Keri Day and Religious Resistance to Neoliberalism — 130
Prophetic Critique — 135
Humanizing Praxis — 148

Postlude: With Love Must Come Hope — 166
Further Theological Considerations — 166
Overcoming Neoliberalism: A Realistic Possibility? — 169
A Love That Produces Hope — 172

Index — 177

Acknowledgments

While my name is on the cover and title page of this book, there are countless people who contributed to the process that led to the following words making it to paper (physical or digital). While there are too many to name, I'll do my best.

First, I must thank the teachers who have guided me through my education at Mount St. Mary's University, Marquette University, and Boston College. Specifically, I'd like to thank Mike Miller, Richard Buck, Thane Naberhaus, and Bill Collinge at the Mount for believing in my potential as an undergraduate, knowing one day I would be able to join them as a colleague. From Marquette, I owe a debt of gratitude to Robert M. Doran, S.J. (1939–2021), and John Thiede, S.J., who aided me in my transition from philosopher to theologian proper and introducing me to Ignacio Ellacuría and Bernard Lonergan, two of my guiding lights. Finally, I must thank my other two guiding lights, M. Shawn Copeland and Andrew Prevot, both of whom mentored and advised me through my doctoral work. Andrew and Shawn, I would not be the thinker, scholar, and teacher I am today without you. I will be ever in your debt.

Next, I would like to thank my colleagues at Mount St. Mary's University and Marymount University, whose support and encouragement as I balanced my high teaching load with writing were essential throughout the process. I am also indebted to my friends, who buoyed me through both the highs and lows of working through this text. Specifically, I would like to thank a few people for their contributions: Aimee Hein, Brian Acton, and Brian Bajzek. Aimee, your support for me and my work goes back to when we met in Boston and has never yielded. Thank you for reading everything I sent you and offering honest, affirming feedback. Brian A., you've been a wonderful conversation partner since we were undergrads, and you've been there for me from my wedding to my dissertation defense. Thank you for offering your expertise in economics when I had questions; it has been of immeasurable help with this project. Brian B., our friendship is one of the most important relationships in my life, and our contemplative walk conversations are always inspiring. Thank you for reading through the entire outline of the project and talking through the argument with me over the course of the two years I spent writing. Again, all three of you have made this book infinitely better.

I would also like to thank my editor, Thomas Hermans-Webster, who has been incredibly supportive through the entire process and has believed in this project since I first proposed it over dinner in Fairfield years ago. Thank you for your efforts, Tom, and I hope this has not been too heavy a burden.

I must also thank my parents, Steve and Theresa Vink. Mom and Dad, you taught me what it means to love and care about others in a meaningful way. This book would not exist without these values you instilled in me. Next, my in-laws, Russ, Laura, and Caitie: you've loved me dearly since I married your daughter and sister a decade and a half ago. Thank you for helping to keep me going during this journey.

Finally, I would like to thank my family. To my beloved son, Bobby: your smile and unbridled joy keeps me going when the road is difficult. Thank you for always being there with a smile, a hug, and a kiss. I heart you so much. Last, and certainly not least, my dear wife, Elisabeth, to whom this work is dedicated: you have walked every step of this journey alongside me with nothing but love and faith in my abilities and the need for this project. Our marriage and your endless love have taught me that with love must come hope. Thank you for everything. I will never be able to thank you enough.

PRELUDE

A Missing Hope

> I got a job working construction for the Johnstown Company, but lately there ain't been much work on account of the economy. Now all them things that seemed so important, well, mister, they vanished right into the air. Now I act like I don't remember; Mary acts like she don't care.... All those memories come back to haunt me; they haunt me like a curse. Is a dream a lie if it don't come true or is it something worse?
>
> —Bruce Springsteen, "The River"

In the year 2000, at the start of a new millennium, there was a great deal of hope in the Global North, particularly in Western Europe and the United States. The victory of the capitalist West over the communism of Soviet Russia opened up new markets for global trade. Liberal democracy was becoming the main form of government in most of the world. In terms of technology, the new possibilities afforded by rapidly developing technologies, especially the spread of internet connections and cellular phones, were pointing us in a direction for greater connectivity. Economically, the increase on Wall Street gave the appearance of growth that would never end, which would eventually reach the businesses and workers on Main Street.

In short, there was hope to be found in every corner and in every heart. After a century that brought economic catastrophe, death, destruction, and untold suffering, the page was turning; a new chapter, defined by peace and prosperity, was on the horizon.

Twenty-five years later, that hope has diminished significantly. The fragile peace was shattered by the 9/11 attacks and the subsequent invasion of Afghanistan by the United States in 2001. The economic crisis of 2007–2008 caused by subprime mortgages led to financial ruin for many people, including the loss of their homes. The internet and the development of smartphones has made connectivity very real, but they have also caused significant damage in our social sphere. The promise of a better future was empty.

Admittedly, this is a very high, bird's-eye view of the situation, but the data regarding people's experiences bear this out. The numbers of people who are suffering from depression and anxiety are on the rise. Wages have stagnated over the last forty-five years, which has led to families struggling to make ends meet, even in two-income households. A significant number of people who went to college, taking out costly loans with predatory practices to do so, are either unemployed or underemployed. An existential crisis is occurring among many Millennials and members of Generation Z because it seems like there is no hope for a future: the world is on fire, the game is rigged against them, and no one with the power to change the situation seems to care.

The fundamental issue behind these interrelated problems is the lack of genuine hope. This lack is also an understandable reaction to the world right now. When the world appears to be operating at the whims of hedge-fund managers and tech moguls, one can feel lost and without recourse. The dearth of hope has awakened some of our darkest inclinations, which leads to more violence, horror, and a grim political future. It can lead people to embrace radical ideas that damage not only others but also themselves, or perhaps even to fall for lies from those who only seek the power to remake the world in their own image.

Theologically, there are very few words that can do justice to what is happening in our society at this point in time, but one comes to mind immediately: evil. The brokenness of the world that is rooted in sin and injustice comes to fruition in the experience of evil on the levels of vital, social, cultural, and religious values. It is ever present in the world any time we read or watch the news. Perhaps what is even more terrifying, evil is in our everyday lives. The struggles that we face every time the grocery bill gets larger for the same amount of food or our rent skyrockets due to a landlord's greed make this evil present in a concrete way. Evil is no longer an abstract metaphysical concept at this point; it is something that presents itself to us in unavoidable ways.

Before moving any further, a few things must be addressed. With as much clarity as possible, this prelude needs to establish what I am doing and what I am *not* doing in this book. In my experience, setting expectations is essential for productive dialogue on any topic. First and foremost, this is *not* an exercise in theodicy. The classical problem of evil in the philosophy of religion inevitably leads to questions of theodicy. While these conversations are important within that realm of inquiry, I have no interest in engaging with those arguments. My primary reason for this is that these arguments do not adequately address one of the central concerns highlighted above: the systemic lack of hope in the culture of the Global North, particularly the United States.

If there is a philosophical investigation that resonates with this project, it would be the work of Gabriel Marcel. In his essay "The Experience of Evil," Marcel considers the existential threat that evil presents and what it does to us on an individual level.[1] Marcel points in the direction I seek to go and has been, admittedly, an important influence in my intellectual formation. While Marcel's work is helpful, his philosophical approach does not provide the theological framework that is necessary to develop the kind of political theology I build in the following pages.

In terms of whose ideas I do work with, I find myself shaped by three twentieth- and twenty-first-century theologians: M. Shawn Copeland, Robert M. Doran, S.J., and Ignacio Ellacuría, S.J. This trinity of thinkers has embraced and interpreted the Catholic intellectual tradition in their own ways, providing fertile ground for my constructive work to take root. Copeland's reflections on suffering, evil, discipleship, and praxis play a large role in the arguments that follow. Her methodological reflections, however, are of the greatest import. Her 2004 presidential address to the Catholic Theological Society of America, "Political Theology as Interruptive," shapes my approach to the theological task. Doran, sharing Copeland's background in the thought of Bernard Lonergan, develops Lonergan's scale of values in a way that allows me to engage with Paul VI's *Populorum progressio* in a productive manner. Also, psychic conversion, the contribution that Doran makes in relation to Lonergan's understanding of cognitional structure, is important for the first chapter of this book.

Ellacuría bears the largest influence on the following work. His liberative political theology blends philosophical precision, systematic theological concerns, and prophetic ethical critiques into a foundation that can be used to read the signs of the times. Given Ellacuría's martyrdom shortly after his fifty-ninth birthday, his work is left unfinished. This project is a development and transposition of his work. In terms of development, my argu-

---

1. For a longer engagement with Marcel as well as the phenomenologist Edmund Husserl, see Andrew T. Vink, "In the Midst of Our Sorrows: An Existential Phenomenology of Evil," *Heythrop Journal* 56 (2015): 15–31.

ments build on the foundation that Ellacuría laid throughout his corpus, bringing in sources that developed after his death to further refine his ideas. By bringing Ellacuría into conversation with the likes of Copeland, I am able to synthesize new insights regarding how the world has developed in the three-and-a-half decades since Ellacuría's death. Through these insights, Ellacuría's project continues to live beyond his death and contribute to a world that is deeply in need of his wisdom.

As for transposition, I must acknowledge a significant difference in context. Ellacuría wrote while serving the people of El Salvador during the turbulent years leading up to and during the Salvadoran Civil War; I am an academic who has lived in the United States my entire life in relative comfort. I have worked menial jobs and experienced precarious financial situations, certainly, but my privilege must be acknowledged. The transposition of Ellacuría's thought into a key that harmonizes with my identity is important; it allows me to make sense of the world of my experience and the concepts that I have engaged with throughout my life when my own cultural framework has failed to help me do so.

This is not to say that Ellacuría's thought, even transposed, does not challenge basic assumptions of American consciousness and worldview. The underlying premises of living in a world and culture shaped by the privilege of the wealthiest country in the world must be brought to light and challenged explicitly. Only by bringing these ideas to light will one be able to address the lack of hope that is present in our society.

There are two key concepts from Ellacuría that are at work throughout the book, though I use their formal names only occasionally: ideologization and historicization. While the terms themselves are not significantly important for this project, the concepts behind them are. We will, therefore, take the time here to explore these interconnected concepts to ensure a firm grasp of how they function both independently and together.

Ideologization

To understand ideologization, we need to understand precisely what Ellacuría means by ideology. In the essay "The Liberating Function of Philosophy," he offers the following definition of ideology:

> a coherent, comprehensive and evaluative explanation through concepts, symbols, images, references, etc., which goes beyond simple, fragmented observation, both in narrow areas and especially in more general and even all-embracing ideas.[2]

In other words, ideology is the way that we make sense of the world, cultivating meaning from our experiences so that it is more than a jumble of sense data. This method of meaning-making, in turn, forms us, reinforcing the way we interpret the world.

Language and culture are examples of this meaning-making. Language allows us to derive meaning from symbols and images that we understand as written language, sounds that convey ideas and concepts in terms of the spoken word, and a system of grammar and syntax that allows for clarity in communication. Our language goes on to form us, shaping the way we decide whether a set of symbols has a meaning that we can discern or not. For example, a native English speaker will read the word "science" and have a fairly clear and particular understanding of the concept. On the other hand, the complexity of the term *Wissenschaft* makes no sense unless the person has a familiarity with German.

Culture is an even better example of ideology, because it includes language and expands it into a wider sphere. Take the example of the current dominant U.S. American culture; it sub-

---

2. Ignacio Ellacuría, "The Liberating Function of Philosophy," in *Ignacio Ellacuría: Essays on History, Liberation, and Salvation*, ed. Michael E. Lee (Maryknoll, NY: Orbis Books, 2013), 93–119, 98.

sumes the English language as part of the wider culture while adding extra meaning to particular symbols. For example, the image of the U.S. flag or the first six notes of "The Star-Spangled Banner" convey a culturally expected sense of patriotism and respect. The culture, then, forms the way in which we view the world. We are shaped to view things through a specific U.S. lens, with concepts of personal liberties, enterprise, democratic ideals, and self-reliance as reference points (for better or worse). We make judgments based on these reference points, and the cycle continues.

It is important to note that, for Ellacuría, ideology is a neutral term. As opposed to the negative connotations that our contemporary language implies, Ellacuría's understanding of ideology is that it is simply a fact of human life and consciousness. Ideology is not something to be condemned but rather a necessary construct that allows one to make sense of the world around them. So long as the ideology presents reality to one's consciousness, there is nothing inherently wrong with it.

The problem emerges, however, when an ideology fails to represent reality. This is what Ellacuría refers to as ideologization. "It unconsciously and unintentionally expresses visions of reality that, rather than manifesting the reality, hide and deform it with the appearance of truth because of interests shaped by classes or social, ethnic, political, and/or religious groups."[3] A particularly dangerous aspect of ideologization is its unconscious and unintentional nature; one never makes a mindful, concerted effort. Instead, it comes upon us unsuspectingly, informing our understanding of the world around us, which, in turn, impacts our choices of action and inaction. Ideologization becomes fundamental for the critical apparatus of our minds and can have disastrous consequences.

---

3. Ellacuría, "The Liberating Function of Philosophy," 99.

Ellacuría highlights five main elements of ideologization. First, it is a totalizing vision of reality that hides a fundamental falsehood or injustice. Second, ideologization has a collective character that expresses itself in a public or impersonal manner. Third, there is an unconscious response to the interests of this collective character that determines what ideas are expressed, not expressed, and deformed. Fourth, the ideologization is presented as the truth by both those who initiate the ideologization and those who perpetuate it. Fifth, an ideologization is presented as a universal and necessary principle, even though it always points to concrete examples that are subsumed into general formulations.[4]

Perhaps one of the clearest examples of ideologization at work in contemporary U.S. society is the "All Lives Matter" movement, the infamous response to #BlackLivesMatter. Following the first criterion, the "All Lives Matter" ideologization proclaims this universal idea that shapes proposed action while ignoring the unjust reality of the white supremacy at work in U.S. society that results in the lives of African Americans being treated as inconsequential and unworthy of genuine concern. The collective nature of "All Lives Matter" fulfills the second criterion, and its deliberate refusal to acknowledge the realities of racial injustice in American society serves as an example of the third. The universal nature of the claims made under the banner of "All Lives Matter" takes them as absolute, universal truths that reframe events in ways that deny the reality of white supremacism, checking off criteria four and five. It is clear, therefore, from Ellacuría's criteria, that we can call "All Lives Matter" an ideologization that deforms one's apprehension of reality, particularly of how the lives of African Americans are undervalued, if valued at all, in the United States.

---

4. Ellacuría, "The Liberating Function of Philosophy," 99.

Historicization

While ideologization subsumes the concrete into an all-encompassing abstract theory, historicization returns the conversation to the concrete details in conjunction with praxis, or thoughtfully considered action. In his essay "The Liberating Function of Philosophy," Ellacuría explains the key ideas underlying historicization in the following way:

> The liberating function of philosophy, which implies the liberation of philosophy itself from all ideologizing participation, and at the same time the liberation of those who are subjected to domination, can only be fully developed by keeping in mind and participating in the historical praxes of liberation. It is difficult for philosophy to constitute itself as philosophy separated from these praxes; but it is even more difficult for it to be liberating or much less as contributing in a real way to liberation.[5]

These two sentences emphasize historical praxes, an engagement with reality where we as humans come into contact with reality. For Ellacuría, human beings are historical animals oriented toward praxis. We are grounded in a historical reality in which our choices and the choices of those who came before us shape the world around us. By bringing this historical aspect to the forefront, the lies and hidden truths at the core of ideologization are revealed for what they are: the cornerstones of injustices at work in various systems that dominate and oppress groups that have been marginalized. Historicization allows us to be critical of our ideologies, interrogating them to ensure that they have not turned into ideologizations. Once ideologization is identified, historicization then moves on to praxis, which enables us to work toward healing the damage done by ideologization.

---

5. Ellacuría, "The Liberating Function of Philosophy," 119.

To make this process more concrete, let us return to the example of "All Lives Matter." If we begin to consider the historical details—the events that took place due to human action or inaction—inconsistencies begin to emerge. We can look to the murder of George Floyd by a police officer in Minneapolis on May 25, 2020, as one example. Floyd's murder by asphyxiation was recorded by cellphone camera, in all its horror, for the world to see. One can see Floyd, already restrained in his arrest, repeatedly gasping out "I can't breathe," while the police officer in question kneels on Floyd's neck.

The example of George Floyd is but one among countless other people of color whose lives ended because their fundamental human dignity was ignored. The names Breonna Taylor, Michael Brown, Freddie Gray, Ahmaud Arbery, Trayvon Martin, and Elijah McClain join the chorus of those whose unjust deaths require the response "Black Lives Matter," while the platitude of "All Lives Matter" rings hollow in its lack of a conviction for justice and respect for inherent human dignity. By telling their stories and addressing the concrete details of their tragic and unnecessary[6] deaths, the ideologization of the "All Lives Matter" becomes apparent. While it is certainly true that every human life is precious, from conception to natural death, because every human being is made in the image and likeness of God, the ideological thrust behind the "All Lives Matter" movement does not actually embody such an idea. "All Lives Matter" is a disingenuous response to a genuine call for justice.

Using the framework of ideologization and historicization to reflect on the various elements of social sin and evil that move

---

6. It is worth noting here that I am using the concept of necessity in the ordinary sense of the term, not using Ellacuría's technical conceptions of the term. Ellacuría would be quick to point out that the aforementioned murders were historically necessary given the social frameworks developed by white supremacy, which we will discuss at length in Chapter 2.

A Missing Hope

throughout our society is very helpful; it can bring insight into the unfathomable amounts of suffering in our world, both visible and invisible. One particular strength of this intellectual framework is its attention to the societal elements of these problems, an attention that tends to be overlooked in many considerations of evil. Through recognizing these societal elements, one is able to truly understand precisely what constitutes the common evil.

The Journey Ahead

The following project proceeds in four chapters. The first chapter engages the common good as integral human development, developing out of Pope Paul VI's work in *Populorum progressio*. From this work, I identify integral human needs, which are necessary conditions for the possibility of human flourishing. I reframe Ellacuría's concept of *el mal común*, the common evil, as integral dehumanization, serving as a concrete counterpoint to the common good and its integral human needs.

The second chapter explores the soteriological implications of the common evil. Ellacuría argued that Jesus's mission was to realize, or bring into reality, the Reign of God, and I argue that the common evil is an obstruction to this realization. The common evil, in its various manifestations, prevents God's plan for the universe from flourishing. This idea comes into focus in and is embodied in the existence of the crucified peoples of history. Part of the Christian vocation—partaking in the grace that allows us to contribute to Jesus's saving work—is, in the words of Jon Sobrino, to take the crucified peoples down from their crosses. We accomplish this through a humanizing praxis: an intelligent and effective action that is rooted in solidarity in which one embraces the social grace that makes such action possible.

The third chapter develops a politico-theological method that can appropriately address the common evil. Building on

Ellacuría's work in "Utopia and Propheticism in Latin America,"[7] I highlight the problematic binary spectrums that allow dangerous ideologizations to continue, providing false solutions to the suffering of the masses. This method, the political theology of dissent, seeks to historicize and allow for healing; by rejecting the binaries that lead to the integral dehumanization, one can then properly discern the injustices, appropriately articulate the necessary prophetic critique, and engage in humanizing praxis that can begin to heal the damage done by the common evil.

Finally, the fourth chapter engages one of the predominant forms of integral dehumanization impacting our world: the politico-economic-cultural structure called neoliberalism. This "unnamed ideology," as George Monbiot so eloquently put it, has contributed greatly to the integral dehumanization of so many members of our human family, in both the Global South and the Global North. An ideologization that transcends the left/right binary of contemporary politics in the U.S. context, neoliberalism has dehumanized the way we understand ourselves as human beings, the way we relate to one another, and the way we understand our responsibility to the wider human community. Throughout this chapter, I move through the steps of the political theology of dissent, ending with suggestions for how to engage in a humanizing praxis that pushes back against this form of the common evil.

In the end, I am seeking the hope that was promised us. That hope, I believe, is necessary if we are to survive the current moment. That hope is a necessary condition for human flourishing. That hope begins with the common good.

---

7. Ignacio Ellacuría, "Utopia and Propheticism from Latin America: A Concrete Essay in Historical Soteriology," in J. Matthew Ashley, Kevin F. Burke, S.J., and Rodolfo Cardenal, S.J., eds., *A Grammar of Justice: The Legacy of Ignacio Ellacuría* (Maryknoll, NY: Orbis Books, 2014), 7–55.

1

The Common Evil

> Now there are varieties of gifts, but the same Spirit; and there are varieties of services, but the same Lord; and there are varieties of activities, but it is the same God who activates all of them in everyone. To each is given the manifestation of the Spirit for the common good.
>
> 1 Corinthians 12: 4–7

To make sense of our faltering society and body politic, we must engage head on the realities of the common evil at work in our world. This is no simple task; the common evil is intricate, daunting, and requires, at times, painful self-examination. Part of this process is a reflection on the common good, one of the central concepts within the Catholic social tradition. By interrogating these concepts, a diagnostic framework emerges that will provide some answers for the malaise infecting our contemporary social and political reality. We can discern a successful praxis for addressing the concrete realities of the poor and marginalized in our world only by considering the common good and the common evil in dialectic tension.

This chapter begins with a discussion of the common good as articulated in *Gaudium et spes*, which provides a cornerstone for this reflection. Paul VI's integral human development and

Robert M. Doran, S.J.,'s articulation of the scale of values are complementary frameworks that support this discussion. From there, I explore Ignacio Ellacuría, S.J.,'s concept *el mal común*, or the common evil. Ellacuría's development of this concept provides a stark contrast to the common good, offering a constructive critique that builds on the tradition and provides a new critical edge. Finally, I offer a new constructive position, framing the common evil as integral dehumanization. This frame focuses our attention on the center stage, where we can explore the common evil and its theological implications in the following chapters.

Articulating the Common Good

The Catholic tradition is rich with ethical and theological articulations of the common good. For our work here, the definition provided by the Second Vatican Council in *Gaudium et spes* stands as an agreeable starting point.[1] Understanding the necessity to engage with the modern world by developing the tradition, the council fathers articulated the common good in a way that speaks to contemporary sensibilities, which makes it easier to build upon contemporary theoretical frameworks. They define the common good in §26:

> Every day human interdependence grows more tightly drawn and spreads by degrees over the whole world. As a result the common good, that is, the sum of those conditions of social life which allow social groups and their individual members relatively thorough and ready access

---

1. I recognize there is a long history of the common good in ethics that I am not including in this investigation. The reason for this is that it goes well beyond the scope of this project. It is not a history of the development of the common good, nor is it intended to be. I am primarily concerned with contemporary theological concepts, and Vatican II serves as a reasonable starting point for those discussions.

to their own fulfillment, today takes on an increasingly universal complexion and consequently involves rights and duties with respect to the whole human race. Every social group must take account of the needs and legitimate aspirations of other groups, and even of the general welfare of the entire human family.[2]

Though concise as our starting point, this definition needs to be unpacked. First, note that the council fathers recognize an essential duality in the human person: we are both individual and social creatures. As individuals, we have concrete needs and desires, dreams and hopes, passions and inspirations that do not match perfectly with any other person. This individuality can and must be respected; the human person cannot be expected to fit a uniform mold that erases their unique features. On the other hand, humans are inherently social. We live in communities, as small as nuclear families and as large as nation-states. We collaborate, share meals, and experience the miracle of life in relation to one another. To deny either aspect is to reduce the human person to something incomplete.

Second, the phrasing of the common good in terms of the "sum total of those conditions of social life" highlights two more insights into the nature of the human person. After establishing the individual/social duality in human persons, the council fathers highlight that human fulfillment comes through the social. One can only be fulfilled through a social reality.[3] We cannot find complete fulfillment, or flourishing to use Aristote-

---

2. *Gaudium et spes* (December 7, 1965), §26 (hereafter cited as *GS*), https://www.vatican.va/archive/hist_councils/ii_vatican_council/documents/vat-ii_const_19651207_gaudium-et-spes_en.html.

3. This runs contrary to the ideals of rugged individualism and self-sufficiency that pervade U.S. culture. This dissonance will be discussed further in Chapters 3 and 4, but it is worth noting this particular challenge within the U.S. context.

lian language, without engaging in some form of community. In addition, fulfillment cannot be reduced to a single condition; a multiplicity of elements are necessary conditions for human fulfillment. To say that only one specific need will allow the human person to flourish is to be reductive. We are complex beings that must be fulfilled on multiple levels to be able to flourish.

Finally, the document defines the common good as a universal pursuit. It is not sectarian but, rather, is to be respected by other groups given how the particular needs of various communities differ according to context. This common pursuit should foster collaboration among social groups through sharing resources to address each community's unique needs. Rather than inspire competition over resources that can turn to violence, there is an inherent obligation in the rights and corresponding responsibilities of all human persons to assist one another in pursuit of the common good.[4] Put another way: the common good raises the standard of living for everyone, and, as such, it requires collaboration that is grounded in friendship and respect. It is a universal vocation for all human beings, who have been created in the image and likeness of God, to work toward this universal fulfillment as we are our sibling's keeper (Genesis 4).

To flesh out this universal human fulfillment, I propose five categories of integral human needs that will allow us to have a clearer sense of the complexity that this implies. The first of these categories is *physical needs*: the basic things a human being requires to survive, such as food, water, housing, medical attention, and so forth. Second are *psychological needs*, or the ele-

---

4. The language of rights and responsibilities comes from the U.S. Conference of Catholic Bishops' seven principles of Catholic social teaching. For further elaboration, see https://www.usccb.org/beliefs-and-teachings/what-we-believe/catholic-social-teaching/seven-themes-of-catholic-social-teaching.

ments required to maintain a healthy sense of self that is capable of interacting with others in a positive way. Examples of this include a recognition of basic human dignity and autonomy, a supportive environment, and access to mental health services to maintain a healthy mental state. The third category is *social needs*. Human beings, as social creatures, require community to thrive. This means that we need to develop communities that are grounded in friendship, respect, and collaboration in order to allow all to flourish. An economy is a concrete example of a social need. An economy is the means by which a community raises the standard of living for everyone. Other examples include social gatherings, athletic events, and a positive group identity. The fourth category of needs is *intellectual needs*: the things that expand and satisfy the human intellect. This group would include accessible education in various forms—formal academic settings, trade apprenticeships, libraries—that consists of artistic endeavors, such as literature, music, visual and performing arts, and other opportunities that help one to explore one's curiosity. Finally, there are *spiritual needs*. As the council fathers identify, human beings are spiritual creatures, and, to follow theologian Karl Rahner's language, we seek transcendence, whether it be through formal religions or other paths that speak to one's inclinations. There are, therefore, needs associated with our spiritual nature that are part and parcel of human fulfillment. In terms of the Catholic tradition, this would include engagement with the sacraments, prayer, and a faith community with which we can celebrate the joy of the gospel and work toward the realization of the Reign of God. The boundaries between these categories are fluid, and some aspects can fit within multiple categories, such as how a faith community can contribute to both social and spiritual needs.

Returning to *Gaudium et spes*, it is clear that the council fathers, focusing on the principles but not the practice, provided very little detail on how to enact these high-minded ideals. This is not a failure on the part of the council; rather, doing so provides a starting point that the tradition may further develop and allows other theological voices to offer their nuances to the conversation. In this spirit, it makes sense that we must go beyond the council's definition to find further insight into the common good.

Following closely on the heels of the council, Paul VI offered his own expansion on the concept of the common good. In his work, Paul VI responds both to Vatican II and to the United Nations proclaiming the 1960s "The Decade of Development."[5] Concerned with a possible reductionist vision of the human person, Paul VI wrote *Populorum progressio* to offer a new vision of development that builds on Vatican II's understanding of the common good. Paul VI's vision in this encyclical is referred to as integral human development—a recognition of the human person's complex web of needs that cannot be reduced to a single element. He writes, "To be authentic, [development] must be well-rounded; it must foster the development of each man and of the whole man."[6] This closely aligns with the definition of the common good found in *Gaudium et spes* and develops the implications for the individual who operates with the abovementioned social groups. This authentic human development

---

5. For more, see Bernard V. Brady, *Essential Catholic Social Thought*, 2nd ed. (Maryknoll, NY: Orbis Books, 2017), 158–59. The phenomenon of developmentalism is also addressed by Gustavo Gutiérrez in the particular context of Latin America, highlighting the way the attitude of development as solely an economic concept only creates further economic inequality and marginalization of the poor. For further detail, see Gustavo Gutiérrez, *A Theology of Liberation*, ed. Sister Caridad Inda and John Eagleson (Maryknoll, NY: Orbis Books, 1988), 13–17.

6. Pope Paul VI, *Populorum progressio* (March 26, 1967), §14 (hereafter cited as *PP*), https://www.vatican.va/content/paul-vi/en/encyclicals/documents/hf_p-vi_enc_26031967_populorum.html.

can be understood as the litmus test for the common good: if authentic human development is not addressed, then the project does not seek to further the common good.

More significantly, Paul VI distinguished categories of "truly human conditions" and "less than human conditions" to be considered through integral human development. At this point, we begin to have a slightly more specific understanding of the conditions of social life mentioned in *Gaudium et spes* and how they may or may not be oriented toward the common good. In *PP*, §21, entitled "The Scale of Values," Paul VI offers an account, albeit short, of these two sets of conditions. He first discusses less-than-human conditions, dividing them into three categories: material poverty, moral poverty, and oppressive political structures. Material poverty, as the name suggests, deals with the lack of material goods for "the bare necessity of life." This list includes food with nutritional value, clear drinking water, secure and stable housing, and climate-appropriate clothing and footwear, among other material needs.[7]

Second, Paul VI identifies moral poverty as "being crushed" under one's self-love.[8] There are a few interesting implications here. He alludes to self-love as the core of moral poverty and, therefore, as the fundamental motivation for immoral activity. When one's self-love is so great, to the point that it becomes destructive, it eliminates the freedom to act with love of neighbor, as the Gospel commands (Luke 10). It also blinds us to the needs of others and inhibits our perception of the world around us to the point that, even if one may be willing to act, one is blinded to the needs of others. Finally, this overgrown self-love limits our empathy by creating a gap between oneself and others that can be difficult to overcome. This leads to a failure to connect with others and see Jesus in the face of one's neighbor.

---

7. *PP*, §21.
8. *PP*, §21.

Oppressive social structures conclude Paul VI's list. He highlights two primary forms of oppressive structures: the abuse of power in authority and the exploitation of workers.[9] This highlights the political and the economic as the primary structures that can be abused. From this statement, one can connect a critique of power structures in light of moral poverty and material poverty. Individuals in a state of moral poverty create and make use of oppressive social structures, which create material poverty and therefore the suffering experienced by the poor and the marginalized.[10]

This leads to another question: what, then, are "truly human conditions"? Paul VI offers various levels of truly human conditions that build on one another. To begin, one must acquire the basic necessities of life, eliminate social ills, expand one's horizons of knowledge, and acquire refinement and culture.[11] On a second level, there is the development of "a growing awareness of other people's dignity, a taste for the spirit of poverty, an active interest in the common good, and a desire for peace." He then acknowledges the "highest values and God Himself," before concluding with the acquisition of faith.[12]

---

9. *PP*, §21.

10. This basic framework will be important as we establish a theory of integral dehumanization below.

11. The language of the acquisition of culture and refinement can be read in two ways. On the one hand, it can be read as the development of literature and the arts, allowing for human beings to move beyond the horizons of mere survival. On the other hand, it can be read as a colonial claim, arguing for Indigenous populations to accept Western cultural norms out of a sense of superiority. I can only speculate at Paul's intention here and therefore offer nothing substantial. For the sake of this project and a hermeneutic of charity, I am choosing to interpret this language in the former manner. Cultural goods are not exclusive to the Global North, and any society that is able to explore these facets of human experience should be celebrated for moving beyond the struggle for basic survival.

12. *PP*, §21.

To help concretize these conditions, let us reframe this hierarchy in terms of the five integral needs of human fulfillment outlined above. Paul VI's first level addresses physical, social, and intellectual needs. The second level considers psychological and some social needs, while the third and fourth levels highlight spiritual needs. Framing the truly human conditions in light of these needs provides some groundwork for finding concrete ways to fulfill these conditions.

In the same vein of the above critique of *Gaudium et spes*, Paul VI highlights lofty ideals for which one should strive, but he provides little in the way of concrete, actionable suggestions. This is again understandable given the universal audience and how such suggestions require a much narrower focus and attention to context. Even so, there is more work to be done in order to make the call to action in *Populorum progressio* viable and actionable.

Robert Doran, S.J.'s work can be interpreted as a parallel system for developing the structure of the common good. Building on Bernard Lonergan's understanding of the good, Doran offers a discussion of the integral scale of values. This structure is helpful for our reflection on the common good in that it provides a formalized structure for understanding the various values that the common good promotes.

Following Lonergan, Doran highlights five levels of value: vital, social, cultural, personal, and religious. These values are then structured in a system such that these values interact in a way that corruption in one level leads to systemic failure in the values below it. For example, a corruption in cultural values—failing to have an appropriate concern for the impoverished—leads to a corruption in social values—the social order that supports the distribution of vital goods—which leads to a failure to properly distribute vital goods.[13] Violence and corruption

---

13. Robert M. Doran, *Theology and the Dialectics of History* (Toronto: University of Toronto Press, 1990), 94–96.

can be healed through grace and self-transcendence, which moves from the top (religious values) to the bottom (personal to cultural to social to vital values). On the other hand, creativity, spurred on by human authenticity, begins with vital values and moves up the superstructure of values, which leads to moments of conversion and self-transcendence.

Doran's expansion of Lonergan is significant not in the details of how the structure of the integral scale of values is further developed but rather in understanding that these values interact in a structured way. For the model of integral human needs, the manner in which a particular category of needs is or is not met impacts the ability to meet another set of needs. For example, the failure to meet one's physical needs, such as proper nutrition, impacts the ability for one's intellectual needs to be met. When a student comes into my university class deprived of proper nutrition, whether due to food insecurity in general or a lack of access to nutritious food specifically, they are unable to learn to their full capacity. When this circumstance is applied to the reality of a child attending elementary school, the stakes dramatically change. A child's development at such a young age is endangered in a way that their ability to attain full human flourishing may be diminished.

While Doran and Lonergan understand the integral scale of values as a hierarchy that highlights each level's significance, the scale of values could be interpreted as placing greater stock in religious values than the others, including vital values. Considering the Gospel's call to bring good news to the poor (Luke 4), it would be better to articulate the system in a way that offers an unequivocally strong emphasis on physical needs.[14] Within the

---

14. Doran offers a response to this critique in Chapter 5 of *Theology and the Dialectics of History*, arguing that integral fidelity to the scale of values requires a recognition of both healing (top-down) and creating (bottom-

framework of integral human needs, each need is both dependent on and supportive of the other four. Emphasizing the interconnected nature of all five human needs better reflects the way that the common good is supposed to operate as the sum total of goods, which are, by definition, interconnected.

Throughout this first section, we have examined three perspectives that develop our understanding of the common good in the context of the latter half of the twentieth century. Beginning with the definition of the common good offered in *Gaudium et spes*, a general framework is established for the way in which the common good would be understood in postconciliar Catholic Social Thought. Its definition, while operating in abstract concepts, provides a starting point for reflection that provides room for growth and development. Next, Paul VI offers a further expansion with integral human development, specifically citing a distinction between truly human conditions and less-than-human conditions. By beginning to hone in on specific categories, Paul VI moves us closer to a concrete understanding of the common good. Finally, Doran offers an integral structure in the scale of values that allows us to see how the various goods interact in a formal structure. While having a potential issue with the hierarchical structure of the scale of values, it nonetheless provides a model for understanding how the common good is grounded in an integration of the various goods as something greater than the sum of its parts.

Throughout this discussion of the various stages of the reflec-

---

up) vectors in the mission of the church. While I am inclined to agree with Doran, the heuristic is still problematic for our purposes here. For more, see Doran, *Theology and the Dialectics of History*, 108–35. Cf. Robert M. Doran, "Suffering Servanthood and the Scale of Values," in *Theological Foundations, Volume II: Theology and Culture* (Milwaukee, WI: Marquette University Press, 1995), 217–58.

tion on the common good, I have also offered my own categories for understanding the common good as integral human needs. The physical, psychological, social, cultural, and spiritual needs of the human person offer a synthesis of the most important aspects of each presentation of the common good in the hopes of providing another heuristic that aids our understanding of how the common good functions in a nonhierarchical form.

There is, however, an important oversight in the discussion of the common good that must be addressed outright. For all its significance, the concept of the common good fails to address the concrete goods, or lack thereof, that are central to seeing the common good at work in the world. While these abstract definitions and expansions are important, they fail to consider the concrete suffering of those for whom the common good is clearly absent. As we move into the next section of the chapter, Ellacuría offers a helpful way to clarify this problem: *el mal común*, or the common evil.

Articulating the Common Evil

At first glance, "the common evil" might seem like an extreme move. To be frank, it is radical; it reframes the entire question from the perspective of what is considered a negative concept within theological discourse. Traditionally, evil has been defined as a privation or lack of that which should be. It has neither substance nor existence in the classical sense. Ellacuría, however, reframes the metaphysical categories of the tradition in terms of historical reality: the experience of human beings as creatures who are historically situated and act in dynamic ways changes history. The evils that human beings experience grant us a level of concreteness that classical formulations of evil shy away from. This concreteness is essential for understanding how "the common evil" provides a necessary counterpoint and complement to the common good, as it addresses the previously stated weaknesses of the concept: the common good's overly abstract and universal nature that can lose the concrete and particular reality of people's suffering.

To begin, let us first look at Ellacuría's definition and explicit critique in understanding the common good.[15] In the essay "Human Rights in a Divided Society," Ellacuría identifies two fundamental assertions that serve as the foundation for the common good:

> Society in the sense of the *polis, civitas*, or political society is a necessary reality for the individual; and society cannot be what it is nor do what it should do if it does not have sufficient material resources at the disposition of all and of each one of its members.[16]

This sets the stage for Ellacuría's concern for the material needs of all members of society. Partly, he is concerned about how the common good tradition will argue that, as individuals are part of the whole of society, particular goods are a part of the whole of the common good. It is clear that acts of selfishness and prioritizing particular goods over and against the common good are wrong, but what happens if a society's common good perpetuates an evil? For Ellacuría, we must ask what happens when there is conflict within a society and the common good for different classes is demonstrably different.

One part of this problem, according to Ellacuría, is the overly

---

15. It is worth noting here that Ellacuría is addressing the longer tradition of the common good, going back to Aristotle and Aquinas. The historical tradition is not fully relevant for the purposes of this project. Ellacuría's interpretation and synthesis of the historical tradition handle critiques of this project not explicitly engaging the entirety of the common good tradition.

16. Ignacio Ellacuría, "Human Rights in a Divided Society," in Alfred Hennelly, S.J., and Johna Langan, S.J., eds., *Human Rights in the Americas: The Struggle for Consensus* (Washington, DC: Georgetown University Press, 1982), 53.

idealistic vision of the *polis*, a flaw dating back to Aristotle. Ellacuría poses the question with the dark reality of slavery in the ancient world:

> Aristotle did not raise nor draw the consequences of the following question: Who were the ones whose material labor made the existence of the free citizens possible? Who constituted the real material base of the city itself and of its common good? In this Aristotelian—and Thomistic—perspective, the common good ceases to be a totality and becomes a partiality, in which not only do all the individuals not share, but a few share because they have prevented others from enjoying what they have produced. The democratic structure and social stratification of Athens and Rome, with their enormous base of slaves, provide a convincing proof of the real denial of the common good.[17]

Ellacuría highlights the idealistic view of society that significant figures within the common good tradition tend to hold. It forgets the underside of history, where the oppressed are usually sacrificed or denied in some way so that the upper class may be free to engage in the fruits of the so-called common good.

The second flaw in the classical argument is an assumption about the nature of law and government. According to the classical tradition, an established order of law, justice, and peace is fundamentally just or, at the very least, necessary to ensure the common good.[18] The reality of totalitarian governments and unjust laws casts this notion into doubt, revealing a fundamental flaw in this assumption. Ellacuría's lived experience in El Salvador throughout the 1970s and 1980s bears this out.[19]

---

17. Ellacuría, "Human Rights in a Divided Society," 57–58.
18. Ellacuría, "Human Rights in a Divided Society," 58.
19. The particular details of Ellacuría's experiences in El Salvador in the decade leading up to his death have been well documented in other works

Beyond the case of El Salvador, the unjust laws of the Jim Crow era in the United States put this conflict on display: newly freed African Americans were constantly hobbled by a variety of laws that prevented them from exercising their constitutionally guaranteed freedoms. It would take another century before these laws would be dismantled by the Civil Rights Act and the Voting Rights Act.

To remedy the idealistic and inaccurate portrayal of reality, Ellacuría offers a method of historicization, where one takes the abstract concept of "how it ought to be" into a given circumstance to see if the necessary conditions for the realization of the concept exist.[20] Historicization, then, provides concrete context and material conditions for a concept to be made manifest in historical reality. It confronts the idealistic tendencies of the common good tradition and provides an honest evaluation of whether or not the common good is possible in a given circumstance. It is a principle of verification that would then allow one to develop a praxis that can attempt to remedy the material conditions that prevent the common good from manifesting in these circumstances.

The key to this methodology, writes Ellacuría, is understanding that this interpretative framework *is* the praxis. In addition to being aware of the disunion between classes or social groups, one must work to identify and overcome the real sources of division. For Ellacuría, a great deal of this work occurs at the socioeconomic level, where the proper distribution of vital goods is key. Disunity has a material cause, and, until that cause

---

and do not need repeating here. For more details, see Teresa Whitfield, *Paying the Price: Ignacio Ellacuría, S.J., and the Murdered Jesuits of El Salvador* (Philidelphia: Temple University Press, 1994); and Robert Lassalle-Klein, *Blood and Ink: Ignacio Ellacuría, Jon Sobrino, and the Jesuit Martyrs of the University of Central America* (Maryknoll, NY: Orbis Books, 2014).

20. Ellacuría, "Human Rights in a Divided Society," 59.

is addressed, full participation in the common good is not possible. The example that Ellacuría gives in this circumstance is international commerce, where the Global North has hoarded resources and deprived the Global South of various goods.[21] True global unity requires a stop to the raging inequality that constantly leaves the global majorities without resources to live fully human lives. The international common good demands equitable socioeconomic relations between various nations and peoples, and the material conditions are not being met.

Ellacuría's final critique is a suspicion of the state. Building on his concern about the flawed assumptions regarding established order, Ellacuría notes that the state presents itself as the formal executor of the common good through laws and rights. Given the failure of established laws and systems of legal justice, the state cannot be trusted in the way that Aristotle and Aquinas argue for. When historicized, the reality of corrupt governments and unjust laws shows that the material conditions for the common good are clearly not met in all situations. This requires a change in material conditions, which is extremely difficult given the number of resources and amount of political will that most governments have to maintain their status quo.

When Ellacuría's critique comes together, the common good seems to be an empty platitude. It appears as a concept without teeth; its meaning can be bent in whatever direction necessary to maintain oppressive structures that support a status quo that brutalizes the poor and the marginalized. With Ellacuría, we must recognize that this empty vision of the common good does not reflect the wealth of the wisdom coming from the tradition. Instead, this impotent stand-in for the common good grows out of a misunderstanding of the integral nature of the common good. Rather than talking only of lofty ideals and broad generalities, we need concrete examples, driven by data that

---

21. Ellacuría, "Human Rights in a Divided Society," 61.

have been gathered through lived experience and engagement with the poor and marginalized communities of the world, to see how the common good is failing to be met. There must be a complementary analysis that can work in concert with the framework of the common good to tell the complete story. Only then will there be sufficient information to guide one's praxis in regard to the suffering of others.

Given this wide-ranging critique, it is clear that an understanding and analysis of the common good alone are insufficient. While the common good is still an essential part of moral discourse, it cannot be the lone category of evaluation, as it does not have the full critical apparatus to provide an adequate analysis. What is the other conceptual tool that we need for sufficient analysis? The common evil.

In *Filosofía de la realidad histórica*, Ellacuría discusses Zubiri's concept of *el pecado histórico*, or historical sin. Ellacuría elaborates on the historicity of sin and how it implies sinful social structures, describing historical sin in the following way:

> A power that is no longer merely enabling, but something that takes over my own life, as belonging to a certain historical moment: there is a historical evil—just as there is undoubtedly a historical goodness, which also has its own power and tends to take control of men—which is there as something objective and is capable of shaping each person's life. It is not just about recognizing the existence of a structural sin, as it is said today, since structural sin is in itself a social sin, something that affects society structurally understood. Historical sin, in addition to being structural, alludes to the formally historical character of that sin: it is a system of possibilities through which the real power of history is conveyed.[22]

---

22. Ignacio Ellacuría, *Filosofía de la realidad histórica* (San Salvador: UCA Editores, 1990), 590. Translation mine.

Ellacuría mentions the phrase *maldad histórica*, historical evil, which Ellacuría scholar Héctor Samour argues is a common evil as such.[23] Let us unpack this further. For Ellacuría, the historical, the social, and the structural are connected. All three of these concepts are rooted in the concrete nature of reality. History, as grounded in reality, is concrete. The social, or the connection between human beings, must be concrete. Structure, which supports concrete realities and organizes them into recognizable patterns, must also be concrete. If this evil is historical, then it is concrete and can manifest itself in and corrupt both social and structural elements of society. Drawing from Doran, the maldistribution of vital goods is one example of this concrete evil: when the structures that allow for the delivery of vital goods and the social values that shape said structures are corrupted, we are forced to engage with a concrete manifestation of the power of evil that can take over a person's life. Suffering is the end result of this evil and is a concrete reality that must be addressed.

According to Samour, the greater argument that Ellacuría is making is against evil as a problem that can be solved by the natural progress of history.[24] Contrary to an optimistic, progressive view of history, evil is not something that will eventually dissipate after decades of progress, in which new advances in science and technology will solve such issues. This Enlightenment mentality ignores the very real ways that technological progress has created new manifestations of evil. Industrialization created new technological marvels, but it also created inhumane working conditions, such as child labor, absurdly long working days,

---

23. Héctor Samour, "The Concept of Common Evil and a Critique of the Civilization of Capital," in J. Matthew Ashley, Kevin F. Burke, S.J., and Rodolfo Cardenal, S.J., eds., *A Grammar of Justice: The Legacy of Ignacio Ellacuría* (Maryknoll, NY: Orbis Books, 2014), 205–13, 208.

24. Samour, "The Concept of Common Evil," 208.

and improper compensation. It would take decades of work by labor unions and activists to overcome these immoral labor practices via legislation. Evil is, instead, overcome by human praxis, which intervenes in historical events to alter possibilities and negates the evil in the present moment.[25] Without this immediate, relevant action, suffering at the hands of historical evil continues unmitigated. The poor and the marginalized are not in a position to wait for things to get better. There must be a dynamic intervention into history via praxis, which Ellacuría claims is the vocation of the human person.[26]

When Ellacuría revisited this idea in a lecture in June 1989, his language changed, challenging the idealized vision of the common good that I have discussed above. Ellacuría began by highlighting the point that the common good cannot be sufficiently achieved if it is expressed only in abstraction.[27] Achieving the common good is not a matter of simply the deduction of abstract principles; it requires a thorough understanding of the material needs and situation of a community whose good one is trying to achieve. For example, the needs of the unhoused population in San Francisco are going to differ from those of the poor of San Salvador, given the different contexts of culture, governmental policies, and laws, even if there are common elements, namely, the need for stable and safe shelter. This is, in part, due to Ellacuría's focus on reality, which has a necessary material component, as mentioned above.

---

25. Ellacuría, *Filosofía de realidad histórica*, 446. Cf. Samour, "The Concept of Common Evil," 208.

26. There are soteriological implications in this statement, namely, a condemnation of a mentality that all of history's problems will be solved at the Second Coming, therefore justifying inaction in the here and now. This will be explored further in the next chapter.

27. Ignacio Ellacuría, "El mal común y los derechos humanos," in *Escritos filosóficos III*, ed. Carlos Molinas Velásquez (San Salvador: UCA Editores, 2001), 447–50, 447.

The emphasis on the contextual particulars of a given circumstance also severely limits the idea of universally applicable actions, which, once again, operate from a point of abstraction. This kind of thinking led to the phenomena of developmentalism and dependency in Latin America, which in large part exacerbated already existing inequalities. This is a lesson we in the Global North still need to learn today: our natural response of simply throwing money at a problem does not address the material conditions and societal conflicts at the heart of these circumstances.[28] Universal principles must be filtered through the context of each community's needs, social structures, and tendencies toward particular harmful practices to ensure that actions taken do not create worse circumstances than those prior to one's intervention. To quote Ellacuría, "Universalization must result from the preferential option for the poor, for the universalization resulting from the preferential option for the rich and powerful has brought more ill than good to humanity."[29] The preferential option for the poor is always expressed in the particular, making it a starting point for a universalism that can address the concrete concerns of those in the midst of suffering. Only when we begin in the particularity of the poor can we then seek to emulate and approximate God's love and mercy in shared, collective action on a broad scale.

---

28. This is not to say that proper funding would not help; the buying power of the U.S. dollar is still something that can make a difference. It must, however, be directed at concrete issues with measures put in place to ensure the money is spent for the goals intended. The details of how this should be done are beyond the scope of my expertise, but a significant part of the failures of funding in Latin America were due to a mismanagement of funds, making it a relevant point of discussion for praxis.

29. Ignacio Ellacuría, "Utopia and Propheticism from Latin America: A Concrete Essay in Historical Soteriology," in J. Matthew Ashley, Kevin F. Burke, S.J., and Rodolfo Cardenal, S.J., eds., *A Grammar of Justice: The Legacy of Ignacio Ellacuría* (Maryknoll, NY: Orbis Books, 2014), 7–55, 25.

Rather than focus only on the common good, which he claims is not a concrete reality for the poor majorities, Ellacuría chooses to focus on the common evil. He defines the common evil as an evil that impacts the majority of a community. Ellacuría's example of malnourished children in both Africa and El Salvador represents the underlying conditions for defining a common evil.[30] First, this malnutrition impacts the majority of the communities mentioned, which is what "common" means in this context. The common evil is a shared experience that goes beyond an individual's suffering. Instead of dismissing one's unique experiences of suffering, "the common evil" expands our account of evil in two major ways. It creates a bond within the community grounded in this shared experience. This bond can bring a community together, even in lament, which in turn allows them to weather the storm of their suffering the best they can. Also, it intensifies the verification that this evil is real and realized. This language of "realized evil" confirms the reality that what *should be* is lacking; there is something that the community requires in order to flourish that it is missing.

Second, Ellacuría's example addresses an explicit evil: depriving children, women, and men of necessary nourishment. The evil should be able to be named. Being able to name the evil avoids the tendency to move evil to an abstract concept that is considered in logical conundrums regarding the nature of God. The suffering that the children, women, and men who are deprived of food experience is not an abstract concept; it is very real suffering. It calls upon our empathy and solidarity, beginning with naming the evil that causes this suffering. Once it is named, the evil loses its mystery and some of its power, providing a focal point for the praxis that is required. To paraphrase fantasy author Ursula K. Le Guin, there is power in the

---

30. Ellacuría, "El mal común," 448.

names of things. With this power, human beings are capable of acting thoughtfully, carefully, and intently to alleviate the suffering of others.

His example also provides an unenumerated element that, for Ellacuría, undergirds the other two enumerated elements: a systematic, structural injustice. While individual instances of suffering can come from a variety of sources—whether it be the malintent of another individual, natural causes such as disease and disastrous weather events, or even something as simple as bad luck—the suffering caused by the common evil is something structural and leads to recurring circumstances that perpetuate this suffering. As Ellacuría notes, the reason that children are malnourished in El Salvador is not because there is no food in the country but because the vital goods that are within the country already are improperly distributed.[31] Corruption like this can occur throughout the scale of values, according to Doran, which leads to these concrete systems of suffering. Another explanation can be seen in Pope John Paul II's discussion of super-development in *Solicitudo rei socialis*.[32] Regardless of the explanatory system that one may derive from the tradition, the sinful social structures that have been put in place via corruption of personal, cultural, and social values perpetuate the common evil. These unjust structures enrich the few while dehumanizing those who are deprived of their daily bread.[33]

Dehumanization is the focal point of Ellacuría's concerns. The common evil, regardless of its form, is a structural injustice that treats the majority as if they lack inherent dignity as human

---

31. Ellacuría, "El mal común," 448–49.
32. John Paul II, *Solicitudo rei socialis* (December 30, 1987) 28 (hereafter SRS), https://www.vatican.va/content/john-paul-ii/en/encyclicals/documents/hf_jp-ii_enc_30121987_sollicitudo-rei-socialis.html.
33. Ellacuría, "El mal común," 449. Cf. Samour, "The Concept of Common Evil," 209.

The Common Evil

beings. Ellacuría highlights capitalism as one such structural injustice. This can be a jarring statement to those of us in the Global North, where capitalist systems have worked to our benefit. In Latin America, however, a very different picture takes shape. Ellacuría writes:

> The problem is not just that of the foreign debt or the exploitation of raw materials or the search for third-world sites to dispose of the wastes of all sorts that the more developed countries produce. More than that, it is an almost irresistible pull toward a profound dehumanization as an intrinsic part of the capitalist system: abusive and/or superficial and alienating ways of seeking one's own security and happiness by means of private accumulation, of consumption, and of entertainment; submission to the laws of the consumer market promoted by advertising—in effect, sheer propaganda—in every kind of activity, including the cultural; and a manifest lack of solidarity in the individual, the family and the state with regard to other individuals, families, or states.[34]

While the specifics of the problems of capitalism will not be relevant for this book until the fourth chapter, I want us to focus on Ellacuría's emphasis on dehumanization in this selection. When a person or a group of people are dehumanized, we lose the ability to bond with them in a meaningful way. The way one relates to a dehumanized person fundamentally changes, especially if one is dehumanized oneself. In the example of the capitalist framework, the human person is reduced to an economic unit that can be manipulated and guided toward choices that enrich a select few while leaving the person in question into the status of economic loss, which further dehumanizes them in the eyes

---

34. Ellacuría, "Utopia and Propheticism," 20.

of the market structure. The bonds, then, that can be used as support during experiences of suffering wither away, and make meaningful relationships extremely difficult, if not impossible. When a community is divided and the inherent human dignity of part of this community is trampled upon by oppressive forces, the common evil is present and must be overcome.

Throughout this section, we have examined Ellacuría's argument for why reflection on the common good alone is insufficient. The concept of the common evil emerges from a concept of historical sin as a counterpoint and complement to the common good as an ethical analytic tool. This provides a context to critique the common good as not addressing the concrete and particular issues that most face today in their states of suffering. The common evil also addresses the flawed assumption of common good theorists regarding the relationship of the state to the common good. The notion of the common evil provides a fuller picture of the status quo because it is an effective analytic tool in conversation with concept of the common good.

The Common Evil as Integral Dehumanization

Ellacuría's discussion of the common evil and dehumanization does not go far enough. We must integrate the language of dehumanization with the concept of the common evil in order to provide the richer exploration of both concepts that Ellacuría seeks to deliver. Given that a significant amount of his writing on this topic was written the year of his martyrdom or left unfinished, one can only speculate how Ellacuría himself would have developed these works further. It is necessary, then, to expand on this framework in a way that honors the work Ellacuría has done while addressing the concerns that have arisen in the three decades since his death.

I propose an expansion of the definition of the common evil beyond an evil that affects the majority of a community.

Instead, I suggest we return to the definition of the common good discussed above to aid in this expansion. Put succinctly, the common good is the set of conditions necessary for the possibility of integral human development. This formulation combines both *Gaudium et spes* and *Populorum progressio* in a way that captures both the spirit of the council and Paul VI's contribution to the development of this doctrine. From this definition, I argue that we should articulate the common evil as that which prevents integral human development, instead instigating and perpetuating integral dehumanization.

To unpack integral dehumanization as a concept, we should take cues from Paul VI, Doran, and Ellacuría: the key element of evil is the privation of that which allows for human flourishing. Evil, then, is that which dehumanizes. Dehumanization can occur in many ways, specifically in how various basic human needs fail to be met. I propose that, if we are to understand the common evil as integral dehumanization, it would be articulated best through a discussion of the failure to meet the five integral human needs addressed at the beginning of the chapter: physical, psychological, social, intellectual, and spiritual. These needs show the complexity of human flourishing, making it relatively easy to see how the failure to meet any of these needs can create a spiral of dehumanization that leads to misery and suffering.

Before diving into a full discussion of what the failure to meet these integral basic needs looks like, we should address the connections between these forms of dehumanization. Considering these needs are integral, the failure to meet them will also be integral. There are resonances between the various forms of dehumanization. I choose the term resonance here because the dehumanization that occurs with each need is a unique form of dehumanization that can also have its presence felt in other areas. The way in which a person is dehumanized takes a different modality depending on the need that is being deprived, but the result is the impediment of human flourishing. This impediment manifests in suffering. These connections are important and will be explored further in later chapters, but, at the moment, the more pressing task is to outline each form of dehumanization in its own right.

Each of these brief discussions of the five forms of dehumanization follows a pattern. First, I provide a basic definition of concrete acts and circumstances that create the impediment to the aspect of integral human development. Second, I provide examples of how this occurs on a communal scale and fulfills the "common" requirement in common evil. Finally, allowing for a fuller consideration of how to properly engage in praxis in this regard, I discuss the unjust structures that perpetuate circumstances.

Physical Dehumanization

Physical dehumanization is perhaps the easiest of the five aspects of integral dehumanization to identify and reflect upon. Physical needs are easy to identify: nutritious food, potable water, consistently available and reliable shelter, climate appropriate clothing, and medical care, to name a few. Denying any of these to a human is dehumanizing. We can even see this in the parable of the Good Samaritan in Luke 10, where the priest and Levite see their fellow Jew beaten to the brink of death, and they deny him basic medical care that would sustain him until he could be seen by a physician of some kind. In this moment, not only are these two religious figures violating Torah's command to love one's neighbor as oneself (Leviticus 19), but they are also actively dehumanizing this person, ignoring their shared humanity for unknown reasons. Only the Samaritan recognizes the dying man's humanity enough to provide the necessary medical care. This is but one example from the Gospels that challenges this form of dehumanization and provides a firm foundation for this critique.

On a wider scale, physical violence as described in the parable from Luke is an obvious example. There are, however, other issues that pertain more to the denial of the concrete needs discussed above. In the previous section, I briefly mentioned the unhoused population of San Francisco. As of 2022, the San Francisco government counted over 7,700 people who were unhoused in the city, with approximately 43.5 percent staying in shelters.[35] While circumstances that lead people to be unhoused vary from person to person, those circumstances do not negate one's inherent dignity as a human being who has been made in the image and likeness of God. This dignity includes one's right to consistently available and reliable shelter. The dehumanization is compounded with the way that most businesses place barriers for unhoused people to fulfill basic needs, such as using the restroom, with policies such as "restrooms for customers only." Hostile architecture, such as spiked grates or benches with armrests in the middle used to prevent a person from lying down on that surface, further compounds the dehumanization by creating inhospitable locations for unhoused people in the name of order and public safety.[36] This sends a very particular message: you are not deserving of this place for rest. We deny you this basic need.

When reflecting on this particular manifestation of the common evil, one must also consider the structural problems that create the conditions for the possibility of this kind of situation. When considering the challenge of the unhoused living in San

---

35. City of San Francisco Government, "Homeless Population," https://www.sf.gov/data--homeless-population.

36. For examples in New York City, see Winnie Hu, "'Hostile Architecture': How Public Spaces Keep the Public Out," *New York Times*, November 8, 2019.

Francisco, we see that part of the problem is an economic one: according to CNBC writer Mike Winters, San Francisco has the third highest cost of living in the United States, behind New York City and Honolulu.[37] It is very likely that this high cost of living makes it very difficult for people in financially precarious situations to handle unexpected events, such as job loss or a large medical bill. With the average rent price in San Francisco as of January 2023 coming in at $3,224 per month, it follows that the number of people in such a precarious position is fairly high, which leads to the large number of unhoused people in the area.[38] Economic structures surrounding housing and other vital goods play a significant role in physical dehumanization. This also needs to be paired with the clear failures of governments at local, state, and federal levels to address this crisis in a meaningful way.

The reality is that physical dehumanization inevitably leads to death. There is no way around this. If people cannot eat, have shelter, or receive medical care, they will die. Especially considering the U.S. context, one of the wealthiest nations on the planet, the fact that people die of exposure and hunger is an outrageous injustice. This does not mitigate the crises of the Global South but highlights the fundamental dehumanizing attitude of this culture. The resources exist to solve these problems, but they are not used in ways that promote the common good. Instead, they embody a common evil that must be addressed.

---

37. Mike Winters, "The fifteen U.S. cities with the highest cost of living—San Francisco Isn't No. 1," CNBC, https://www.cnbc.com/2023/08/22/us-cities-with-the-highest-cost-of-living.html.

38. Sami Sparber and Megan Rose Dickey, "San Francisco Area Rents Still Steep among High Demand," Axios San Francisco, January 31, 2023, https://www.axios.com/local/san-francisco/2023/01/31/san-francisco-high-rent-apartments.

Psychological Dehumanization

Psychological dehumanization is best understood as the lack of acknowledgment of fundamental human dignity that impacts the way one views oneself. The compounding concern discussed above is very relevant here because the compounding occurs within one's own psyche. Various forms of abuse, whether in physical or verbal forms, impact the victim's mental state. Abuse victims tend to internalize the violence done to them and begin to see themselves as less than human. This form of dehumanization is particularly insidious because of this internalization. When victims begin to see themselves as less than human, they believe they are deserving of the abuse. They allow the physical and/or emotional violence to continue until it reaches a lethal situation, whether by the abuser or by self-infliction.

Psychological dehumanization does not necessarily come from abuse. It can also develop from untreated mental illness and the consequences that come along with that. People struggling with depression, for example, can have intrusive thoughts that are inherently dehumanizing, leading to a similar downward spiral that can lead to suicidal ideation and attempts at self-harm. Jessica Coblentz, inspired by the work of phenomenologist Martin Heidegger, describes depression as "unhomelikeness," where one experiences a profound displacement and loss of connection to the world that those without depression take for granted.[39] This experience of displacement can feed into a sense of isolation with intrusive thoughts that compound these feelings, leading to a separation from the feeling of being human. If one does not feel at home in the world inhabited by human beings, is it not natural that one would question one's own humanity?

---

39. Jessica Coblentz, *Dust in the Blood: A Theology of Life with Depression* (Collegeville, MN: Liturgical Press Academic, 2022), 38–39.

Both of these examples can have tragic consequences regardless of whether the instigation of the dehumanization is external or internal. Psychological dehumanization is important and worthy of attention, though it is fraught with stigma. Only after decades of ignoring or mistreating mental health issues are we at a point where the conversation regarding psychological dehumanization can take place.

Suicide among transgender youth is a clear example of the common element of psychological dehumanization today. According to a study in *Journal of Interpersonal Violence*, 56 percent of transgender youth have attempted suicide, while 86 percent have reported experiences of suicidality. Among contributing factors, interpersonal microaggressions, school belonging, emotional neglect by family, and internalized self-stigma all had statistically significant impacts on their experience.[40] This reality shows a manifestation of the common evil, impacting the vast majority of transgender youth and highlighting a particular failure of our society to show the love and mercy to which we have been called by none other than Jesus.[41]

This leads to the next question: what are the working structures that enable psychological dehumanization to continue? Considering the way psychological dehumanization is intertwined with mental health, the best way to address this problem is from the perspective of access to mental-health care. This is

---

40. Ashley Austin, Shelley L. Craig, Sandra D'Souza, and Lauren B. McInroy, "Suicidality among Transgender Youth: Elucidating the Role of Interpersonal Risk Factors," *Journal of Interpersonal Violence* 37, nos. 5–6 NP2696–NP2718, https://doi.org/10.1177/0886260520915554.

41. For a more robust theological account of the topic of the marginalization of transgender people in conjunction with other groups, see M. Shawn Copeland, "Marking the Body of Jesus, the Body of Christ," in *Knowing Christ Crucified: The Witness of African American Religious Experience* (Maryknoll, NY: Orbis Books, 2018), 61–80.

not to say that mental-health care is the silver bullet to psychological dehumanization; rather, it can be a lifeline to those in the throes of this kind of suffering. To answer this question, consider two different unjust structures that impede access to this form of health care: the cultural and the bureaucratic.

The cultural structure is the more familiar of the two. Contemporary U.S. culture does not consider the impacts of mental health on the well-being of its members. Between nonexistent work/life boundaries, socially acceptable cruelty, and an overall denial of the reality of the integrated human being needing more than the bare necessities of survival, contemporary U.S. culture does not encourage any of us to have concern for mental health. It insists that we ignore problems, keep hustling, and "look on the bright side." These are empty platitudes at best and dangerous practices at worst.

The bureaucratic structure is rooted in the complicated web of the U.S. health insurance system. Journalist Kate Woodsome highlights the failure of the U.S. health insurance system to adequately allow for patients to receive the care they seek. This failure is primarily due to bureaucratic obstacles such as prior authorizations, insufficient reimbursement to providers, and "unacceptable limits on care."[42] Given that the U.S. health insurance system is a multi-billion-dollar industry, there is little incentive for those who run insurance companies to make the necessary changes that are required by law.[43] As opposed to increasing access to necessary mental-health care, these companies limit access and allow this manifestation of the common evil to proliferate.

---

42. Kate Woodsome, "Health Insurance Is Keeping Your Mind Sick and Your Wallet Empty," *Washington Post*, July 21, 2023. While Woodsome's article here is an opinion piece, it links to several studies and news articles that serve as evidence for her argument.

43. Woodsome, "Health Insurance Is Keeping Your Mind Sick."

Social Dehumanization

Social dehumanization can be understood in two ways: the individual in relation to a social group (class, ethnic identity, national identity, etc.) and the smaller social group in relation to a larger group. The individual form of social dehumanization has a significant number of resonances with the psychological dehumanization in light of the impact of interpersonal relationships on psychological states. Even so, the greater mechanism at work behind social dehumanization links the individual and small group situations through the scapegoating mechanism.

Scapegoating, according to cultural theorist René Girard, is the replacement of a guilty party with an innocent party who then takes the blame and punishment for the guilty party's actions. In other words, it is victim substitution in the face of violence. Comparing victim substitution with sacrificial offerings, Girard writes:

> In a world where violence is no longer subject to ritual and is the object of strict prohibitions, anger and resentment cannot or dare not, as a rule, satisfy their appetites on whatever object directly arouses them. The kick the employee doesn't dare give his boss, he will give his dog when he returns home for the evening. Or maybe he will mistreat his wife and his children, without fully realizing that he is treating them as "scapegoats." Victims substituted for the real target are the equivalent of sacrificial victims in distant times. In talking about this kind of phenomenon, we spontaneously utilize the expression "scapegoat."[44]

Within the context of social relationships, Girard's work on scapegoating helps us easily to imagine how a group may select a specific individual (or a larger group select a smaller group)

---

44. René Girard, *I See Satan Fall Like Lightning*, trans. James G. Williams (Maryknoll, NY: Orbis Books, 2001), 156.

to blame for issues unrelated to that individual/smaller group. Such victim substitution makes it impossible for the individual or smaller group to integrate and form a community. This leads to many possible dehumanizing circumstances, such as second-class citizenship, apartheid, total ostracization, or even genocide if the conditions make it a possibility.

The examples of the evils caused by this social dehumanization are, unfortunately, far too many to count. From the Shoah to the Armenian genocide to the Rwandan genocide, there have been many examples of genocide in world history. On a smaller but no less serious scale, the Jim Crow laws and lynchings in the United States and the struggles of women in various cultures around the world reveal the commonness of second-class citizenry, worker exploitation, and dehumanization as acts of victim substitution. Each of these examples is applicable at both group identity and individual levels for members of the victimized group.

The structures that underlie social dehumanization depend on the biases of the people who build these structures: white supremacy, antisemitism, sexism, xenophobia, Islamophobia, and homophobia, to name a few. This kind of group bias becomes formalized in and foundational for social structures through legislation, corporate policies, and overall cultural attitudes that continuously victimize groups who are deemed to be prime candidates for victim substitution.

I must emphasize that victim substitution occurs only when innocent parties are involved. When a social group chooses to ostracize an individual, such as a Neo-Nazi, for their harmful beliefs and actions, such ostracization is acceptable because the party is guilty. Karl Popper's paradox of tolerance is in effect at this point.[45] Can one ostracize a guilty party in a dehumanizing

---

45. The paradox of tolerance, first articulated by Karl Popper, shows the tension in creating a truly tolerant society. Per Popper, a completely tolerant

fashion? Of course, yes. Not all ostracization is dehumanizing, however, particularly when there is just cause.

Unfortunately, victim substitution continues to serve as the foundation of social dehumanization, in part because people do not want to address the root causes of their frustration. Dismantling institutionalized structures of discrimination is itself an onerous task, and it begins with the difficult work of self-reflection and conversion. Still, until these elements are brought to task, social dehumanization will persistently manifest the common evil.

Intellectual Dehumanization

Perhaps the most unexpected element of this list, intellectual dehumanization deals with the understanding that human beings are inherently rational creatures and our desire to learn is a spark that begins in our infancy. To quote Lonergan, "The questions of children are simply endless. The problem is to teach them that the answers to questions are not as easy as they think, and to do so without discouraging and stopping the flow of questions."[46] One is dehumanized when this fundamental need to ask questions and accumulate knowledge is hindered or even prevented because one's rational nature is not acknowledged and respected. Intellectual dehumanization also impacts one's ability to fully engage in society as a member of the body politic and contributes to social structures that maintain many instantiations of the common evil.

---

society must be tolerant of intolerant ideas, such as antisemitism or xenophobia. Once such intolerant ideas come into play in an open society, these intolerant ideas tend to gain steam and take over the society. A truly tolerant society, therefore, must be intolerant of intolerance to protect itself as a tolerant society. For more, see Karl Popper, *The Open Society and Its Enemies* (London: Routledge, 2011).

46. Bernard Lonergan, *Topics in Education*, ed. Robert M. Doran and Frederick Crowe (Toronto: University of Toronto Press, 1993), 104.

A wide-ranging education that provides a foundation for understanding how the world and society function is one of the necessary elements of human development. In the Western tradition, this takes the form of the liberal arts education: a student studies the humanities, natural and social sciences, and the arts regardless of one's major in collegiate education or focus in precollegiate education. By doing so, a graduate will be prepared to understand complex issues, parse information, and make sound judgments related to public life. When this skill set is not properly developed or forgone completely, it becomes nearly impossible to fulfill fully one's role as a citizen in a democratic state. It is dehumanizing also because we are, to paraphrase Aristotle's *Politics*, political creatures: we desire to engage in the work of civic life to allow for the possibility of flourishing.[47] Depriving the innate intellectual inclinations and the ability to fully engage in the political arena strikes at some of the fundamental elements of what make us human. Editing textbooks through censorship is one concrete way in which this is attempted. Using the purchasing power of a city's public education system, one can select a textbook that tells a narrative of history that aligns with one's political leanings at the expense of a holistic picture of past events.[48]

Another element of this intellectual dehumanization is the spread of misinformation, which proliferates faster than ever with social media platforms. When individuals intentionally put out misinformation, they do so with the expectation that its target audience will not have the critical reasoning skills to dis-

---

47. This understanding of the human person is also recognized in the common-good tradition with the focus on participation in public life as a central part of human flourishing.
48. The clearest example of this is in the battle over textbooks used in U.S. public schools. For further analysis, see Dana Goldstein, "Two States. Eight Textbooks. Two American Stories," *New York Times*, January 12, 2020.

tinguish truth from falsehood. This misinformation can then go on to shape the body politic in a way that pushes an agenda that is reliant on a misrepresentation of some kind of data. In other words, misinformers expect that the population is a group of fools who are easily tricked and misdirected; misinformation assumes that the target audience is somehow less than human.

The structures that support this kind of dehumanization are those that are dependent on the dysfunction of the democratic state. If the body politic is unable to perform its democratic duties, there is a power vacuum that allows for the possibility of antidemocratic politicking to occur. There can be explicitly antidemocratic governing through authoritarian policies and motivations, where one may use executive power for one's own gain and magnification of power. There can also be an implicit antidemocratic politicking by means of economic power. Those with the most political capital, accrued through campaign donations or personal wealth, influence governing structures to have laws written in a certain way that benefits their fortunes. This all comes from the presumption that the voting population is not smart enough to figure out the game and the manner in which they are manipulated. This dehumanization resonates on both the individual and social level, creating yet another form of the common evil.

Spiritual Dehumanization

Finally, we must discuss the way spiritual dehumanization promotes the common evil. Spiritual dehumanization occurs when a person's spiritual life, whatever form that may take, is violated or denied them through violence. One way this occurs is the reduction of the human person to merely a material unit, which can take many forms. When the human person is truncated to just an economic unit or just an animal with developed intellect, one's spiritual capacity, whether it be expressed through organized religion or independent, personal spirituality, is denied. Cultural forces can be at work here, as well as a failure of religious traditions to address the needs of the population, making people feel as though there is no need for spiritual guidance or development.

A second way in which spiritual dehumanization takes place is through spiritual abuse. This form of spiritual violence[49] can take two distinct forms: the institution as perpetrator and a representative of the institution as perpetrator. In the former case, the institution performs acts that explicitly deprive a person of a spiritual home or deny their value as made in the image and likeness of God. The open dehumanization of LGBTQ+ persons by a church, denying them a place at the table where they can be involved in the full life of the church community, is a concrete example of this first form.[50] This kind of decision and action is a violent event, seeking to disrupt one's relationship with God. It is a betrayal when one considers the teaching of a loving and merciful God and Jesus's welcoming ministry in the Gospels.

In the latter case, a representative of an institution uses their power and authority to do violence to an individual for the sake

---

49. My use of the term spiritual violence is taken from Theresa Tobin's definition as "a distinct form of violence that uses sacred objects, texts, teachings, or rituals to violate a person in her spiritual self and harm her relationship with God." For further detail, see Theresa Tobin, "Spiritual Violence, Gender, and Sexuality: Implications for Seeking and Dwelling among Some Catholic Women and LGBT Catholics," in Philip J. Rossi, ed., *Seekers and Dwellers: Plurality and Wholeness in a Time of Secularity* (Washington, DC: The Council for Research in Values and Philosophy, 2016), 133–66.

50. I am intentionally leaving this open because there is a fair amount of diversity among Christian church communities on LGBTQ+ issues. Even within the Catholic Church, where magisterial definitions play a role in how one navigates these issues, parishes vary in how welcoming they are of LGBTQ+ persons and their families. While it is undeniably true that a bad experience with one parish can cause a person to turn away from the faith, it can also be the case that a welcoming and loving experience can open one up to the faith once more.

of their own power and gratification. We have seen stories time and time again of bishops, ministers, priests, and other representatives of the church engaging in violent acts against minors or others under their authority, or, equally terrible, covering up these acts of violence so they never see the light of day.[51] These acts of violence once again dehumanize the victims by denying their dignity as human beings and objectifying them as a means of sexual gratification. This kind of violence can have psychological repercussions for the victim as well, creating a resonance with psychological dehumanization.

What structures support this form of dehumanization? Power structures that are created within faith communities that resist the *sensus fidelium*—the sense of the faithful—and its call to create a welcoming and egalitarian community of faith are necessary to support spiritual dehumanization. This is not to take away from the sacramental vocation to Holy Orders. Instead, resisting the *sensus fidelium* is the willful ignorance of the power dynamics at play between the clergy/ministers and their congregations. Only when this clericalist power dynamic is appropriately named and negotiated can healing begin. Until that point, spiritual dehumanization will continue, as will the common evil.

This discussion of the common evil as integral dehumanization can take its full shape only in the recognition of how the denial of the aforementioned five integral human needs work together. Integral dehumanization creates a complicated web of factors that compound a person's dehumanization, which

---

51. Specific examples of this can be seen in the various findings of the *Boston Globe*'s report on sex abuse by clergy from 2001, the Philadelphia grand jury report in 2018 regarding the movement of accused abuser priests, and L'Arche Internationale's 2023 investigation into Jean Vanier's sexual misconduct. There are countless other examples outside of the Catholic tradition as well.

leads to a misery and suffering that one cannot fully explain or make sense of. Even this framework is only a model for trying to understand what is an inherently mysterious concept, with very real consequences for all persons, especially those on the margins of society. Integral dehumanization as a framework for the common evil offers a useful tool for analyzing causes and appreciating the complexity of human suffering that cannot be easily addressed or dismissed.

Conclusion

The common evil as a counterpoint to the common good is a necessary adjustment to ethical reflection built around this framework. By grounding one's reflections in concrete suffering, especially that of the poor and marginalized, the absence of the common good is highlighted in a unique way. It puts the focal point on those to whom Jesus ministered in the Gospels and allows one to reflect on and act within authentic discipleship. Reflecting on the common evil does not diminish the common good tradition in the least but rather provides the modality needed to bring the tradition to a deeper level of self-awareness. Without a reflection on the common evil, the common good rarely touches the concrete reality of suffering populations.

This shift in modality brings with it several other challenges. By engaging with the issue of the common evil as integral dehumanization, questions as to how to go about enacting praxis from this analysis arise. Can one come to a discrete answer that addresses the suffering of others, or is everything tangled in a web of cause and effect that can even double back on itself? Can an outsider's praxis adequately impact someone experiencing psychological dehumanization? Or can only interior praxis on the part of the victim rectify this? These questions and others require consideration and prudent judgment on the part of the one reflecting and seeking to act.

As one might expect, questions of a politico-theological nature arise from this shift to the common evil. Given the political nature of the common good, an analysis of how political systems in a particular context influence the common evil always takes shape in the concrete. As will be discussed in the third chapter, the response to this analysis will take a radical shape, responding to the prophetic call to denounce evil when it is found and provide hope for a better future.

The most pressing theological issue that arises from the shift to the common evil is the question of how this shift influences our theologies of the cross. How do our soteriological reflections on the cross and its implications for those whom Ellacuría called "the crucified people" change when we pay attention to the concrete realities of suffering in our world? If this common evil is present in historical reality, then what does salvation mean for us? From what are we saved if these evils persist? If the inherent dignity of the human person is not only ignored but denigrated in such an overwhelming manner, does salvation have any meaning? Does the common evil mean there was a failure to save? These questions strike at the very heart of the Christian faith and must be answered before any other theological conversation can take place.

2

Obstructing the Reign of God: Soteriological Implications

He said, "Son, when you grow up, would you be the savior of the broken, the beaten, and the damned?"
—My Chemical Romance, "Welcome to the Black Parade"

The common evil as integral dehumanization presents unique challenges to how we traditionally understand salvation in the Christian tradition. Until we reckon with what the common evil means for humanity's active participation in Jesus's saving work, we will never fully understand Jesus's mission. By unraveling these questions, a deeper understanding of how salvation works in history will emerge.

This chapter begins by examining the relationship between Jesus's mission and salvation, providing context to the death and resurrection as the salvific act, through the realization of the Reign of God. Next, I discuss how the Reign can be obstructed by the common evil and its manifestations in various forms of structural sin. Finally, I propose that solidarity is a humanizing practice and a solution to this obstruction. This analysis frames our engagement with Jesus in a collaborative grace to continue the mission of realizing the Reign of God.

Understanding the Reign of God: Salvation of and in History

To begin, we need to establish what precisely we mean by Jesus's mission. Following Ellacuría, I argue that Jesus's mission was to realize the Reign of God. Here, the verb "realize" does not hold its usual definition of coming to understand. Rather, "realize" means to bring into reality; in other words, to make real. The potential for the Reign of God, an ordering of the world grounded in justice and peace rather than power and violence in the greater context of God's gratuitous love, is all around us. The mission of Jesus works toward realizing the Reign; this mission, as discussed below, is the mission to be taken up by the church after the Ascension and Pentecost. This mission is the ideal that leads Jesus through his public ministry, to his eventual passion and resurrection.

Taking Ellacuría and other Latin American theologians such as Gustavo Gutiérrez and Jon Sobrino as our guides, we see that the mission of Jesus is not limited to only the passion and resurrection.[1] It includes his earthly ministry. Significantly for Ellacuría, the earthly mission provides meaning to the following death and resurrection, and vice versa. Only focusing on the death and resurrection, says Ellacuría, ignores the historical context that gave rise to the death and resurrection. Instead, we must see the situation that gave rise to Jesus's death and resurrection.

> Jesus dies—is killed as the four gospels and Acts so insist—because of the historical life he led, a life of deeds and words that those who represented and held the reins

---

1. While we will explore this mostly through the lens of Ellacuría's theology, examples can also be found in Jon Sobrino, *Jesus the Liberator* (Maryknoll, NY: Orbis Books, 1994); and Gustavo Gutiérrez, *A Theology of Liberation* (Maryknoll, NY: Orbis Books, 1988).

of religious, socioeconomic, and political situation could not tolerate. That he was regarded as a blasphemer, one who upset the social structure, a political agitator, and so forth, is simply to recognize from quite distinct angles that the activity, word, and very person of Jesus in the proclamation of the Reign were so assertive and so against the established order and basic institutions that they had to be punished by death. Dehistoricizing this radical reality leads to mystical approaches to the problem, not by way of deepening, but by way of evading.[2]

Ellacuría calls us to recognize that Jesus of Nazareth belonged to a time, place, and culture; these aspects of his personhood cannot be separated from his mission. He reacted to the political status quo of first-century Palestine under the rule of Rome and the *Pax romana*. He understood himself as a Jew and was formed by the teachings of the Hebrew Scriptures. He judged and reacted to religious and social establishments through that formation.

Why, then, does this matter for Jesus's mission? Historicizing Jesus provides the context for how Jesus would carry out his earthly ministry. Who Jesus of Nazareth was as a person, shaped by his historical and social context, dictated how he would go about his mission of realizing the Reign of God. The historical fullness of his personhood explains his following in the footsteps of the prophets, seeking justice for those who are marginalized in society, as the literal incarnation of the preferential option for the poor. Jesus's actions are intended to realize that new divine order, something the powers that be in his time could neither accept nor tolerate.

---

2. Ignacio Ellacuría, "The Crucified People: An Essay in Historical Soteriology," in *Essays on History, Liberation, and Salvation* (Maryknoll, NY: Orbis Books, 2013), 195–224, 206.

Since Jesus's earthly ministry is central to understanding the meaning of the death and resurrection, it is important to identify what that ministry included. For this, Sobrino offers five helpful categories for understanding Jesus's ministry as it is described in the Gospel accounts: miracles, casting out devils, welcoming sinners, parables, and celebrating the coming of the Kingdom of God.[3] These categories provide a framework for understanding what Jesus's context simply would not tolerate. For our purposes, the first and the third categories, miracles and welcoming sinners, are the most important.

Miracles should be understood as liberative, salvific signs for the poor, grounded in Jesus's compassion, showing the closeness of the Kingdom of God.[4] These salvific signs healed, pardoned, and exorcised the poor from their daily suffering, providing hope that the Kingdom of God was at hand and incarnating God's preferential option for the poor. This is an inversion of the social order that cannot be tolerated. The poor are to be pitied but not given preference, even though Jesus's own actions are in keeping with what the Hebrew Scriptures call for.

Welcoming sinners might be even more important. Jesus's ministry of hospitality and welcome was truly revolutionary. We see this clearly in the story of Zacchaeus, in which Jesus chooses table fellowship with a notorious tax collector. Jesus's

---

3. Sobrino, *Jesus the Liberator*, 87–104.

4. Sobrino uses the term "pity" here to translate *splagchnizomai*, the Greek term used to describe Jesus's actions. I take issue with this rendering because of the connotation of the word "pity" as looking down on someone. Copeland, on the other hand, uses the word "compassion," which does not have the same connotation issues. Both authors agree that the Greek term provides the same meaning, that Jesus was moved to his core at the plight of the poor, but they render that meaning differently. I prefer Copeland's rendering and will use that throughout, even when using Sobrino's framework, to avoid the connotation issues. For more, see Sobrino, *Jesus the Liberator*, 90–91; and Copeland, *Knowing Christ Crucified*, 174.

welcoming offers salvation both to oppressors and to those who are seen as sinners because of some kind of weakness in the eyes of a strict moral legalism. Sobrino offers the following explanation, highlighting how political Jesus's mission is:

> [Jesus] directly demands a radical conversion of the first group, an active cessation from oppressing. For these, the coming of the Kingdom is above all a radical need to stop being oppressors, although Jesus also offers them the possibility of being saved.... Jesus requires a different kind of conversion from the second group: acceptance of the fact that God is not like the image they have introjected from their oppressors and the ruling religious culture, but true love; that God comes not to condemn but to save, and that sinners should therefore feel not fear but joy at God's coming.[5]

The prophetic call to conversion for each group undermines the socioreligious order. Those in positions of power must wield their power responsibly while sinners must allow themselves to be forgiven in God's loving and accepting embrace. The former call angers those who abuse their power, and the latter call throws into disarray the power dynamic between those deemed righteous and those deemed sinners according to the law. Jesus confounds the order of sin in both calls to conversion, creating an upheaval that cannot be tolerated.

Jesus engaged primarily in religious activity, yet Jesus was crucified under the political framework of the Roman Empire, as the Nicene Creed clearly states.[6] Religious leaders worked to get him noticed by the Roman authorities, however, revealing an inherent link between the religious and the political in the

---

5. Sobrino, *Jesus the Liberator*, 97.
6. Ignacio Ellacuría, *Freedom Made Flesh: The Mission of Christ and His Church*, trans. John Drury (Maryknoll, NY: Orbis Books, 1976), 46.

world. Jesus's mission, therefore, cannot help but be political by its nature.

His religious activity, interpreted politically within the sociopolitical context of Jesus's day, shows that the salvific death and resurrection of Jesus could not have happened without this political element. The mission was necessary to bring about the kind of death that was necessary to complete the salvific act. Jesus's mission, therefore, is as significant for the salvation of humankind as his death and resurrection.

The historical nature of human agency provides further context for the significance of Jesus's mission. Ellacuría's understanding of the human being as a historical being, as one who is oriented toward action in history, helps us more fully recognize this context. Ellacuría scholar Kevin Burke, S.J., offers the following definition of history: "History refers to a distinct human structure comprising both transmission and tradition."[7] This understanding of history implies human action: we transmit things and pass things on via tradition. This means that culture, philosophies, and even basic human interactions move through our actions. If there is transmission and passing on, then there must also be a corresponding reception; that which is passed on must be received. These two actions—passing/transmitting and receiving—develop the structures that frame the rest of human action and create a context for the structure through which each of us experiences reality. This process, as Burke notes, is creative and tied to human freedom. He writes:

> As an essential characteristic of the human, freedom is shaped by the personal, social, and historical dimensions of the human and by the real possibilities from among which it chooses and which, through choice, it shapes and

---

7. Kevin F. Burke, S.J., *The Ground beneath the Cross: The Theology of Ignacio Ellacuría* (Washington, DC: Georgetown University Press, 2000), 83.

passes on. Possibilities become real only insofar as they are handed on by the social body of the human in history. To speak, therefore, of a discrete human freedom detached from society or removed from history is to utter nonsense. Human freedom is personal, social, and historical.[8]

By highlighting this connection between human freedom and the historical, we can notice the way that history forms over the course of time: through human choices. These choices shape history, a fact with which we are already familiar. These structural changes can have impacts on a grand scale by shaping that which is transmitted and passed on. Human beings shape history, and history in turn shapes us.

The historical choices that we make, however, are not always good ones. To quote Burke, "Humans not only make history, they make a mess of history."[9] We destroy as much as we build. We can create wonders that serve as the hallmark of our kindness and generosity while simultaneously engage in acts of cruelty and depravity. The fundamental double-edged sword of freedom is this: one can choose wickedness just as easily as justice. Through irresponsible human choices, we transmit and pass on injustice through social structures that institutionalize dehumanization, thereby embedding dehumanization within the very traditions that we pass down. The legacy of white supremacy in the United States is a clear example of how this happens, and its consequences are discussed in greater detail below.

We need saving from our irresponsibility, which means that salvation must occur within history. This is part of the reason that Jesus's earthly mission is central to the narrative of salvation. His choices, made in line with a sinless human nature,

---

8. Burke, *The Ground beneath the Cross*, 84.
9. Burke, *The Ground beneath the Cross*, 85.

established new structures of justice that his followers were and are still called to engage and pass on within the Christian tradition. Our action in history allows for our active participation in Christ's salvific work. Salvation is not only necessary; it is *historically* necessary.

Here, we ought to pay close attention to an essential distinction between natural necessity and historical necessity. Natural necessity is when an event necessarily occurs without human intervention. As one might surmise, these events occur most notably in the natural world. A clear example of this comes from basic meteorology: when a low-pressure system meets a high-pressure system, a rainstorm occurs. No human action is required to make that happen. Another example comes from the laws of Newtonian physics: for every action, there is an equal and opposite reaction. Again, no human meddling is required. More concisely, one could also think of natural necessity as the way the natural world operates independent of any kind of intervention. Ice melts, apples fall from trees, and caterpillars turn into butterflies. All of these things occur as natural necessity.

Historical necessity, on the other hand, is created not by natural processes but by human action. Historical necessity describes an event or series of events that must take place because of the ways that human actions have shaped the context and situation. One way to understand this is in light of the complexities of presidential elections in the United States. Based on decisions made by the founding fathers, the president of the United States is elected based on votes received by the delegates in the Electoral College from each state, not by the popular vote of the country as a whole. That means that the candidate with the most electoral votes must become president, even if they do not win the popular vote. This situation is created by historical necessity.

Human actions and decisions have consequences. These consequences can shape both the immediate future and future possibilities that may not come to pass for centuries down the line. The presidential election example above shows this clearly. On a theological level, original sin is one of the great examples of historical necessity. Original sin is a fundamental fracture in humanity's relationship with God that has created a world that is grounded in coercive power and violence as a response to any challenge to power.[10] As discussed below, this situation becomes an obstacle for Jesus's mission and causes a conflict that results in Jesus's death. Once we are able to understand this relationship of historical necessity, the role that human beings play in the work of salvation becomes much clearer.

When we recognize the relationship between human actions and historical necessities, we ought to then ask meaningful questions about the soteriological implications of human historicity. There are at least three central themes in these questions.

First, what does continuing Jesus's mission on earth look like after the Ascension? In other words, how does the church fulfill its mission?

Second, what does participation in this mission look like?

Third, how do the answers to the first two questions fit within the context of a historical soteriology?

Ellacuría offers helpful insights to address the first question in the essay "The Church of the Poor, Historical Sacrament of Liberation."[11] This essay outlines how the church should be act-

---

10. The discussion of what constitutes original sin is beyond the scope of this paper. My interpretation of original sin is heavily influenced by the work of James Alison and Daniel Horan, who have both used Girardian mimetic theory, which fits with some of Doran's interpretations of sin and evil. For more, see James Alison, *The Joy of Being Wrong: Original Sin through Easter Eyes* (New York: Herder & Herder, 1998), and Daniel Horan, *Catholicity and Emerging Personhood: A Contemporary Theological Anthropology* (Maryknoll, NY: Orbis Books, 2019).

11. Ignacio Ellacuría, "The Church of the Poor, Historical Sacrament of Liberation," in *Essays on History, Liberation and Salvation* (Maryknoll, NY: Orbis Books, 2013), 227–53.

ing to continue Jesus's mission of realizing the Reign of God. Simply, the church's mission is embodied in its role as the historical sacrament of liberation, as the title of the essay clearly states. If we understand sacraments as the concrete conduits of God's grace to human beings, then the church is to be the concrete conduit of God's grace in a way that affects historical reality and human beings as historical animals. This is not to say that the traditional seven sacraments are not historical in Ellacuría's understanding of the word; rather, the church is uniquely charged, as the Body of Christ, to engage with history in a way that the other sacraments cannot by their very nature. This mission involves an engagement with and transformation of society through means other than abusive and violent power. In keeping with Jesus's own earthly mission, the church's mission involves hospitable subtlety and peaceable nuance. Making the same comparison, Ellacuría offers a helpful analysis:

> Like the mission of Jesus, the mission of the church is not the immediate fulfillment of a political order but the fulfillment of the Reign of God, and, as a part of that fulfillment, the salvation of any existing political order. By political order we mean here the global institutionalization of social relations, the institutional objectification of human actions, which comprises the public venue of their personal and interpersonal actions. The church does not have sufficient corporeality or materiality to bring about the immediate fulfillment of this political organization, which extends to everything from collective knowledge to social organization, from the structures of power to social forces; other entities exist for that purpose.[12]

Ellacuría first highlights that the church herself cannot fix every problem within the political order, nor is she meant to. The

---

12. Ellacuría, "Church of the Poor," 240.

church is to realize the Reign of God, like Jesus, healing and transforming the world in the ways in which she is able so as to establish an order built on justice and peace. Building on justice and peace, the church does not have the material resources to bring immediate fulfillment to the political order as she knows it. Her mission, then, must reflect a prophetic patience and hope. Instead of immediate gratification, the church can and should use her insights and wisdom to identify and challenge the political order through her prophetic office. When the political order has institutionalized dehumanizing practices and relationships, the church's challenge calls forth the members of the Body of Christ to then work to transform the political order so that this dehumanization no longer takes place.

Such prophetic words and actions are not as easy as they may sound. The church is still a group of imperfect people, and those imperfections have consequences. Sometimes, members of the church conflict with one another over an issue, or their personal biases prevent them from seeing the harm that is happening in their midst. This is part of what Ellacuría means when he says the church lacks sufficient materiality: the people that make up the church will never perfect the social order because of our own fallibility. We can, however, help in our imperfect ways by opening potential paths for greater growth and change. Ellacuría uses the metaphor of bread making, describing the world as dough and the church as "salt, which inhibits corruption, and leavening, which transforms the dough from within."[13] Notice that Ellacuría does not say the church is the baker, who kneads the dough into submission, but rather the salt and leavening, which allow the bread to rise of its own natural processes. The church allows the world to grow and develop into its intended form not through coercive power but loving action.

---

13. Ellacuría, "Church of the Poor," 240.

The loving action of the church, like that of Jesus, must emerge from within the poor and the marginalized. According to Ellacuría, this is the very nature of the historical form of love. He writes, "As the word of God is read from this situation of structural sin and structural violence, Christian love presents itself forcefully in terms of the struggle for justice, which liberates and saves crucified and oppressed humanity."[14] When we engage the struggle for justice, we embody the call of the gospel to live according to the order of justice and peace instead of the order of power and violence. So long as we use just means in our struggle to, in Sobrino's language, take the crucified people down from the cross, we live out the historical form of love. The church, therefore, must be a sacrament of liberation for the victims of history, taking them down from their crosses as the order of power and violence erects them in the name of domination and profit. Ellacuría furthers this argument, noting that, for the church of the poor, "poor" can refer not only to the economically rich–poor relationship but also the domination and deprivation that characterize all relationships between the dominated and their oppressors.[15] The church's responsibility, therefore, is to stand with the marginalized and become a conduit for God's grace for those who have been dehumanized, *even if the church has contributed to that marginalization.* She must be an active conduit, giving God's grace a historical form, which can "mean something real and palpable in the life of the poor."[16]

Put succinctly, the church's mission as historical sacrament of liberation is to actively minister to those who have been dehumanized by the world around them. By engaging the struggle for justice and avoiding abuses of power and violent

---

14. Ellacuría, "Church of the Poor," 243.
15. Ellacuría, "Church of the Poor," 247.
16. Ellacuría, "Church of the Poor," 248.

acts, the church actively transmits grace through the historical form of love through selfless acts that are grounded in justice and peace. In pouring herself out for the poor and marginalized, the church emulates Jesus's salvific act, partaking in and continuing Jesus's mission in history.

Now that we have established the church's mission as historical sacrament of liberation, and the salvific connotation of that term, we can move to discuss our participation as historical humans in the continuing mission. One option can be found in reading the tradition, particularly in the work of St. Anselm of Canterbury, through a praxis-focused lens. In her reading of Anselm's *Cur Deus homo*, Lantinx theologian Nancy Pineda-Madrid highlights Anselm's emphasis on the active role of the faithful in his soteriology. She writes, "In order to be saved, human beings must *actively* affirm that Christ died for them; they must recognize Christ as acting in their stead. Salvation demands that humans be in touch with their deepest desire and orientation toward God and that they open themselves to act in accord with this."[17] Pineda-Madrid's concise description of Anselm's emphasis on human activity can be developed in two related ways: one focused on biblical interpretation and application and another focused on the role of human persons in history.

The emphasis on both belief and action can be interpreted as a development of James 2. In James 2:17 we read, "So faith by itself, if it has no works, is dead." Active belief in Jesus's role as savior requires the believer to orient their life toward the actions of Jesus's mission, which are described in the Gospels as acts of mercy. Drawing again from James 2: "If a brother or sister is naked and lacks daily food, and one of you says to them: 'Go in peace; warm yourself and eat your fill,' and yet you do not

---

17. Nancy Pineda-Madrid, *Suffering and Salvation in Ciudad Juárez* (Minneapolis: Fortress Press, 2011), 62.

supply their bodily needs, what is the good of that?" (2:15–16) There must be a harmony between belief and action that reflects one's belief in Jesus and his salvific mission and acts. According to Anselm, by way of Pineda-Madrid, we cannot be passive in our salvation. If we are passive, then Jesus becomes a substitution for humanity rather than one who acts in our stead to do that which is beyond our ability. This is the point of the God-Human for Anselm: to close the infinite gap, which only God's power can do, and make satisfaction, thus restoring order to the universe. Such satisfaction can come only from the initiative of a sinless human being.

New possibilities for our theology and our praxis emerge when we read Anselm's active role for humanity in salvation in conjunction with James 2 and the historical nature of human beings. Recognizing the historical structures that surround us as human beings, a liberationist-informed reading of Anselm calls for us to investigate and engage with the structures of power that create the hungry and the naked, the poor and the marginalized. The influence of human action on the dynamics of history, as discussed above, has wide ranging effects, which means that historical decisions must be addressed so that we can clothe the naked and feed the hungry as well as put forth our efforts toward preventing people from becoming naked and hungry in the first place. Such an approach allows us to live out the faith in the context of our concrete action.

This leads, then, to the second definition of historical soteriology that Ellacuría presented in "The Crucified People." He defined the term as "a matter of seeking where and how the saving action of Jesus was carried out in order to continue it in history."[18] While Jesus's earthly life and death are complete events, the mission continues. So long as humankind lives and

---

18. Ellacuría, "Crucified People," 207.

dies, Jesus's mission continues in "its saving omnipresence."[19] The mission contextualizes the entirety of the paschal mystery, signaling to Christians that the realization of the Reign of God is part of the responsibility of our calling.

We may be tempted to spiritualize this call to continue the mission by focusing only on its spiritual and sacramental elements at the expense of historical actions. Ellacuría pushes back against this fiercely. He writes:

> The continuity is not purely mystical and sacramental, just as his activity on earth was not purely mystical and sacramental. In other words, it is not in the cultic, not even in the celebration of the Eucharist, that is the *totum* of the presence and continuity of Jesus; there must be a continuation in history that realizes what he realized in his life and as he realized it.[20]

The sacramental life of the church is important, but it cannot be the totality of its call. The concrete historical actions of Jesus's mission require action. As discussed above, Jesus healed the sick, ministered to the lowly, and ate with sinners: all concrete actions in history. If we, as Christians, are to follow Jesus and work to realize the Reign of God, then we must also continue these concrete actions in history that gave meaning to his life and death.[21]

Though we should be hopeful that our call to discipleship can be accomplished, the path of Christian discipleship is challenging. The world constantly resists the mission we are called to engage in. We are constantly obstructed by forces that appear to be beyond our control and beyond our understanding. How does the common evil contribute to this obstruction? When we think about the common evil as integral dehumanization, what

---

19. Ellacuría, "Crucified People."
20. Ellacuría, "Crucified People," 207–8.
21. Ellacuría, "Crucified People," 207–8.

insights can help us understand this obstruction and how we must respond to it?

Obstructing the Reign of God: The Common Evil in Action

A reign of sin obstructs the Reign of God. St. Ignatius of Loyola, a foundational figure for Ellacuría's language on the common evil, gives a fuller picture of how the obstruction of the Reign of God is even possible. From the Ignatian roots of this theological analysis, we can explore the obstruction by understanding the reign of sin as the common evil. This exploration includes a brief theoretical discussion of an overall framework and a reflection on three different ways that the common evil manifests as an obstruction of the Reign of God.

In *The Spiritual Exercises* of St. Ignatius of Loyola, the fourth day of the second week provides a meditation on two standards, or battle banners: the Standard of Satan and the Standard of Christ. The image of two standards standing across from each other on a battlefield, awaiting confrontation and contest, is powerful. Of the two, the Standard of Satan is of greater interest to us in this chapter. Ignatius describes the Standard of Satan in the following way:

> Consider the address [Satan] makes to them: How he admonishes them to set up snares and chains; how first they should tempt people to covet riches (as he usually does, at least in most cases), so that they may more easily come to vain honor from the world, and finally to surging pride. In this way, the first step is riches, the second is honor, and the third is pride; and from these three steps the enemy entices them to any other vices.[22]

---

22. Ignatius of Loyola, *The Spiritual Exercises and Selected Works*, ed. George E. Ganss, S.J. (New York: Paulist Press, 1991), 155.

This imaginative exercise still applies in our contemporary society, almost to a T. The drive for riches, honors of the world, and surging pride culminate in a desire for the power to attain those things. The power dynamics behind the desire for the three vices that Ignatius lists offer insight into why one might seek these things. Why does one seek riches? To have the economic power to obtain what she values. Why does one seek honors of the world on top of riches? To have the social power and capital to obtain the things money alone cannot buy. Why surging pride? To justify the things she has done in the name of obtaining those things as worthy of their goal. Inevitably, these three vices lead to dominating power in attempts to satiate the desires that are created by these vices. Dominating power always ends in sin, whether it be on the individual or social level.

When one acts in sin, one creates a situation in which other members of society, whether through direct actions or indirect actions, suffer. With Karl Rahner, we must recognize the direct link between love of God and love of neighbor.[23] If we understand sin to be, at least in part, a violation or rejection of the love of God, then, assuming Rahner to be correct, sin must also be a violation or rejection of the love of neighbor. This violation or rejection breaks down social connections, saying, "You are not worthy of love." Repeated cycles of these actions can build structures that are built on this violation or rejection of love, or sinful social structures.[24]

These sinful social structures and the suffering they cause are historically necessary rather than naturally necessary. For

---

23. Karl Rahner, "Reflections on the Unity of the Love of Neighbour and the Love of God," in *Theological Investigations, Vol. 6* (Baltimore, MD: Helicon Press, 1969), 231–50.

24. Daniel Horan offers an interesting reflection on sinful social structures. For more, see Daniel P. Horan, *Catholicity and Emerging Personhood: A Contemporary Theological Anthropology* (Maryknoll, NY: Orbis Books, 2019), 189–216.

example, the world of first-century, Roman-occupied Palestine was unable to handle Jesus's radical message of justice, peace, and love because of the sins upon which society was built and the sinful social structures that operated within it. This is historical because, as discussed above, human beings are historical creatures and our actions have consequences in the formation of history. The historicity is, in essence, the framework of the reign of sin: sinful social structures function as a result of concrete human action to actively obstruct the love of the Reign of God, thereby leading to widespread suffering.

Dehumanization links the reign of sin and the common evil. The reign of sin depends on domination and an unquenchable thirst for power. This power is taken—and it certainly is taken rather than given freely—through the dehumanization of other members of society. By othering and dehumanizing other members of society, one builds power structures grounded in sin and unjust suffering.

In keeping with Ellacuría's emphasis on the common evil as particular and concrete, we must move beyond theoretical descriptions of the reign of sin and identify the examples we can see at work in our world today. I offer three brief cases that attend to the concrete nature of the reign of sin in distinct contexts: white supremacy as articulated by James H. Cone, the phenomenon of feminicide in Ciudad Juárez as described by Nancy Pineda-Madrid, and how economics and technology can become a tool for dehumanization.

White Supremacy as the Reign of Sin

According to James H. Cone, the key issue in the problem of white supremacy in the U.S. context is not personal prejudice. Rather, the institutionalization of that prejudice, which leaves Black children, women, and men unprotected by the law from

Obstructing the Reign of God   59

racial prejudice, is the crucial issue at hand.[25] White supremacy is fundamentally social. Throughout this book, I work with a functional definition of white supremacy that recognizes white supremacy as the collection of institutionalized racial prejudices that particularly benefits white people as a whole, particularly when those benefits come at the expense of people outside the bounds of whiteness.[26] White supremacy has taken multiple forms in the history of the United States. To paraphrase M. Shawn Copeland, the institution of chattel slavery is perhaps the most pivotal aspect of white supremacy, as it created the world in which we live. It also serves as the clearest example of integral dehumanization on a massive scale: the subjugation of an entire race of people due to the color of their skin, thereby turning them into property. Their lives became mere commodities to their white masters, who traded their enslaved people like livestock. These masters evaluated oppressed children, women, and men for their aptitude for hard labor and good breeding. If chattel slavery does not show a clear picture of integrated dehumanization and the privation of the common good, then nothing can.

While the institution of slavery was eventually made illegal in most cases through amendments to the U.S. Constitution, its legacy lives on.[27] This is part of the sinister nature of white

---

25. James H. Cone, "Theology's Great Sin: Silence in the Face of White Supremacy," in *The Cambridge Companion to Black Theology*, ed. Dwight N. Hopkins and Edward P. Antonio (Cambridge: Cambridge University Press, 2012), 143–55, 147.

26. I acknowledge that this definition is incomplete. If I were to dive into the intricacies of a more robust definition of white supremacy, it would take us far afield from concretizing the reign of sin.

27. It is important to note that the Constitution does not prohibit slavery in the case of convicted criminals. This loophole has created the opportunity for prison systems to use a form of slave labor. It has in turn been used as a tool for white supremacy with the mass incarceration of people of color

supremacy: it continues to make its presence felt through different institutions even as the laws and moral norms around previous manifestations change. The most important manifestation for Cone is the practice of lynching in the Jim Crow era. In the introduction to his seminal work *The Cross and the Lynching Tree*, Cone describes this phenomenon:

> In its heyday, the lynching of black Americans was no secret. It was a public spectacle, often announced in advance in newspapers and over radios, attracting crowds of up to twenty thousand people. An unspeakable crime, it is a memory that most white Americans would prefer to forget. For African Americans the memory of disfigured black bodies "swinging in the southern breeze" is so painful that they, too, try to keep those horrors buried deep down in their consciousness, until, like a dormant volcano, they erupt uncontrollably, causing profound agony and pain. But as with the evils of chattel slavery and Jim Crow segregation, blacks and whites and other Americans who want to understand the true meaning of the American experience need to remember lynching. To forget this atrocity leaves us with a fraudulent perspective of this society and of the meaning of the Christian gospel for this nation.[28]

Lynching is another clear manifestation of integral dehumanization. When the death of Black children, women, and men are celebrated as spectacle and noteworthy events, drawing crowds numbering in the thousands, these children, women, and men are no longer human—they are objects for the entertainment of

---

disproportionate to the makeup of the population. For more on this topic, see Michelle Alexander, *The New Jim Crow: Mass Incarceration in the Age of Colorblindness* (New York: New Press, 2010).

28. James H. Cone, *The Cross and the Lynching Tree* (Maryknoll, NY: Orbis Books, 2011), xiv.

white masses. Furthermore, lynching has not truly disappeared in the twenty-first century. Rather, it has transformed from spectacles for the masses into public executions captured on camera. One only needs to look at the stories of Michael Brown, Trayvon Martin, Breonna Taylor, Tony McDade, George Floyd, and countless others to see that lynching remains a live strategy of violence against Black Americans. Once again, white supremacy shifts its malignant form to another instantiation by blending in with whatever power structure is available. Lynching, regardless of its form or how it is broadcast, is a concrete example of integral dehumanization.

Cone highlights the connection between the lynching tree and the crucifixion, making the significant claim that Jesus was lynched. American Christianity must acknowledge this fact and take shape through this fact. Like practices of chattel slavery and mass incarceration, lynching is a concrete example of white supremacy as integral dehumanization and an active obstruction to the Reign of God. Bringing Cone into dialogue with Ellacuría at this point, the continued lynching of Black children, women, and men condemns American Christianity, for, as Ellacuría points out, we should know better and provide justice for these crucified people. Instead of allowing injustice to prevail, we must take these crucified people down from the cross.[29]

Feminicide as the Reign of Sin

In *Suffering and Salvation in Ciudad Juárez*, Nancy Pineda-Madrid turns our attention to feminicide, the killing of women because they are women. She describes it further:

---

29. As I discuss below, this is not a call to some form of white saviorism. Instead, it is a call to act with mercy in accordance with the divine command of Micah 6:8 to "do justice, and to love kindness, and to walk humbly with your God." By focusing on the prophetic charge in Micah, we can shift from a modality of saviorism to one of fraternal love that acts with compassion.

According to this definition, feminicide builds on femicide but now includes the phenomenon of impunity for the perpetrators because the state is implicated, either explicitly or implicitly, and makes clear that this crime transpires on a large scale, that is, it is widespread and rooted in the structural inequalities that render some women and girls acutely vulnerable. To this I would add one further descriptor, namely, that the killings are exceptionally brutal and vicious, a point exemplified in the case of Ciudad Juárez and several of the other cases listed above.[30]

These killings are rampant in Ciudad Juárez, with victims falling into the cracks created by a society that puts little value on their lives. In Pineda-Madrid's account of victims' stories, she articulates competing interests and how they interact to produce no justice for these women. These interests disregard the safety of the poor and include economic interests, the state's interests, and the interests of dominant social institutions in the area.[31] Each of these interests provides an insight into integral dehumanization, making them complicit in the common evil.

The economic interests in Ciudad Juárez do not prioritize ending the feminicide. As Pineda-Madrid describes, the business opportunities that were created by the North American Free Trade Agreement (NAFTA) drove the owner class in Ciudad Juárez to seek cheap labor they could easily manipulate and exploit. Their ideal target was poor, young, dark-skinned women. They created situations in which women became the breadwinners, therefore willing to accept changes to schedules that forced them into dangerous situations and made them prime prey for those who seek to do them harm.

---

30. Pineda-Madrid, *Suffering and Salvation*, 12.
31. Pineda-Madrid, *Suffering and Salvation*, 28–29.

While I agree with Pineda-Madrid in that NAFTA and globalized capitalism are not the direct causes of the feminicide, the economic narrative regarding the feminicide in this context provides crucial insights into the dehumanization that can result from the priorities of capital generation under this capitalist structure. The need to feed the economic engine is bound up in the necessities of base survival in a capitalist society and forces a dehumanization that values one's livelihood as worth more than their flourishing life. It truncates the human person to one who simply "lives to work," where work is not a life-giving, co-creative activity as John Paul II envisions in *Laborem exercens*. Rather, work becomes a life-draining, dehumanizing task that reshapes the human person as an object that possesses no value outside its productivity. In cases like the ones that Pineda-Madrid details in Ciudad Juárez, it can lead one to take a shift change that puts her in mortal danger.

Economic analysis alone, however, can overemphasize the economic structures in ways that further objectify these women by ignoring their resistance to the situation.[32] There is something to be said of the women who choose to resist the danger and continue to put food on the table for their children. Their courage is humanizing. Pineda-Madrid engages the economic interests at work in order to direct our attention to their courage. In the tension between utter dehumanization and humanizing resistance, we can witness the concrete acts of history amid the seemingly abstract elements of the economic narrative.

In addition to the economic interests, state interests show little urgency to address feminicide, let alone work toward its end. In a just society, all of its members are protected under the law. Should they be violated, the state will intervene to serve justice, for that is its purpose. The problem in Ciudad Juárez,

---

32. Pineda-Madrid, *Suffering and Salvation*, 29–30.

says Pineda-Madrid, is that the state does not seek justice for these victimized women; instead, it seeks only to cover up the embarrassment created for the government and the police force by their impotence in preventing these murders.[33] Instead of owning up to their failures, the government blames the victims, claiming that these women were living double lives as sex workers and, therefore, brought their fate upon themselves.[34] This tactic is social dehumanization at work: by labeling the victims of feminicide as deviants from social norms, the victims are deemed less than human and, therefore, undeserving of justice. Once this dehumanizing narrative takes hold in the wider society, the government's failure to perform one of its most basic responsibilities is ignored and a broken system perpetuates itself. In short, such corrupt systems require social dehumanization to maintain power.[35]

The economic narrative becomes another tactic that the Mexican government uses to avoid responsibility. By blaming the machine of economic progress as the main culprit in feminicide, the state implies that their deaths were inevitable costs in the historic march of economic progress. Simply, the state tries to weave a narrative that economic circumstances led to these women's deaths in an attempt to deny its own failure to protect its citizens. This strategy is not unlike its attempt at blanket victim-blaming. Pineda-Madrid writes:

> The state's role and complicity must be foregrounded, because doing so provides greater clarity on the extreme degree of vulnerability marking the lives of young, poor, dark-skinned women in Ciudad Juárez. In the end, the

---

33. Pineda-Madrid, *Suffering and Salvation*, 30.
34. Pineda-Madrid, *Suffering and Salvation*, 30.
35. This phenomenon could also be understood in Girardian terms as a form of scapegoating. For more on this, see René Girard, *I See Satan Fall Like Lightning*, trans. James G. Williams (Maryknoll, NY: Orbis Books, 2001).

feminicide is a crime of the state "which tolerates the murders of women and neither vigorously investigates the crimes nor holds the killers accountable."[36]

Emphasizing the failure of the state highlights the sociopolitical nature of human beings because it calls our attention to how structures of justice are essential to our expectations of how justice ought to be administered, especially in the context of Western liberal democracies. Within the framework of positive law, we expect that justice will be served in accordance with the severity of the law broken. One would expect murder to deserve a quick and satisfactory punishment. When this justice fails, members of society are left even more vulnerable than they would be otherwise.

Within dehumanizing contexts of gender-based harassment and violence, feminicide itself adds a layer of dehumanization that further obstructs the loving grace of the Reign of God. The failure of earthly justice, particularly in the case of the victims of feminicide, betrays a social dehumanization that further alienates disenfranchised populations, compounding the psychological and physical dehumanization they are likely already facing. This failure is also an obstruction to the Reign of God, which is built on justice and peace.

Digital Technologies as the Reign of Sin

The twenty-first century, with all of its technological wonders and advancement, has created a new form of exclusion in which a lack of access to digital-age technology severely impedes one's ability to function in society. When used as an exclusionary force, digital technologies create further states of dehumanization that can be as frustratingly complex as analog technologies like border walls, weaponry, and chain-link cages for migrant

---

36. Pineda-Madrid, *Suffering and Salvation*, 31.

children. Given the social significance of smartphones, X (formerly Twitter), and augmented reality, a discussion involving lack of internet access as a form of material poverty does not appear in theological literature as prominently as one might expect.[37] This may be in part because internet access is still seen as a luxury product for consumers to use as opposed to a basic utility, like water, heat, and electricity. These utilities, even when privately commodified and managed, are seen as fundamental services to which an individual should have easy and affordable access. Increasingly, however, two elements of internet-based technologies are essential for social inclusion: substantial access and general technological literacy.

Substantial access can be defined as a reliable network that would allow one to access the internet, a reliable device with which to access the internet, and sufficient time to conduct necessary business using the internet, such as homework or job applications. Substantial access stands as an assumption for elementary and secondary education, as well as employment. For example, a *New York Times* article from February 2016 cites the case of the Ruiz family of McAllen, Texas: Tony and Isabella, two middle-school students, are forced to download and do their online homework on the sidewalk outside of their school, barely in range of the school's wireless hotspot, because their family is not in a financial position in which they can afford the internet access necessary to complete the work at home.[38]

---

37. One notable exception is Katherine G. Schmidt, *Virtual Communion: Theology of the Internet and the Catholic Sacramental Imagination* (Lanham, MD: Lexington Books, 2020). In the first chapter, Schmidt addresses the question of access as one of the theological concerns that should be considered when reflecting on the internet and its relationship to society. For more, see *Virtual Communion*, 9–12.

38. Cecilia Kang, "Bridging a Digital Divide That Leaves Schoolchildren Behind," *New York Times*, February 22, 2016, https://www.nytimes.com/2016/02/23/technology/fcc-internet-access-school.html.

The assumption that homework can be done online outside of school at the middle-school level shows that modern society is moving in a direction where a substantial internet connection is not an extra benefit for a child's education. It is a necessity. The COVID-19 pandemic created conditions that only strengthened this claim. In that context, a substantial internet connection was needed even to attend school in the first place.

Beyond education, a substantial internet connection significantly influences the process of applying for jobs. According to an article on the *Huffington Post* from as far back as 2012, an applicant searching for work—regardless if it is for a substitute teaching position or a sales associate position at The Gap—needed to submit their application online.[39] Jamal Mason, of the Bronx, relied on public library computers to apply for jobs, so this form of application posed an obstacle. He was forced to race against the clock to fill out applications to stay within his forty-five-minute time limit at the library.[40] Given that a job application can take anywhere from twenty minutes to ninety minutes to complete, such time restraints make it extremely difficult for someone to make an effective use of their time while in the job market. The expectation of substantial internet access builds on a bias against those who may need the job most. Furthermore, it is now expected that one not only has substantial internet access but also a smartphone with which to access the internet. Even fast-food restaurants such as McDonald's or Taco Bell, some of the most accessible jobs for a person in the job market, require the use of a smartphone's QR code scanner to access a job application. This further puts up a wall for the most vulnerable members

---

39. Gerry Smith, "Without Internet, Urban Poor Fear Being Left Behind in Digital Age," *Huffington Post*, March 1, 2012, http://www.huffingtonpost.com/2012/03/01/internet-access-digital-age_n_1285423.html.

40. Smith, "Without Internet."

of society who attempt to integrate into society through even the most basic form of employment.

The education and employment examples also fit the second criterion of a general technological literacy. General technological literacy can be defined as a group of basic skills needed to effectively do business on the internet, such as access and use email, use word processing software, and format PDF files. Younger students, for example, are given online homework to start developing these skills, but a recently unemployed welder or factory worker who has not needed to use a computer in the two-to-three decades since first entering the workforce may have trouble with these skills. Yet, most jobs that pay a living wage in the U.S. context require a knowledge of these skills, which makes it more difficult for traditionally skilled laborers to make a transition to the new economic situation.

These issues primarily stem from the lack of substantial access, but they require education and training beyond that substantial access. Simply, in the contemporary U.S. context, substantial internet access and general technological literacy are needs that must be met as part of a dignified life. These needs ensure that human persons have the freedom to pursue a fulfilling life free from domination, which Ellacuría argues is essential to the liberative process.[41]

Substantial internet access and technological literacy intersect our exploration of integral dehumanization at the point of isolation. The isolation that is created by the lack of access and technological literacy is a clear example of social dehumanization. It can lead to economic insecurity, a lack of proper education, and an inability to maintain meaningful, stable relationships. Any

---

41. Ignacio Ellacuría, "Utopia and Propheticism from Latin America: A Concrete Essay in Historical Soteriology," in J. Matthew Ashley, Kevin F. Burke, S.J., and Rodolfo Cardenal, S.J., eds., *A Grammar of Justice: The Legacy of Ignacio Ellacuría* (Maryknoll, NY: Orbis Books, 2014), 41.

one of these goes on to impact one's interior life as well, further compounding an integral dehumanization. As mentioned above, while technology can seem like a luxury, the stark reality is that those without access to said "luxury" are treated as second-class citizens at best and not fully human at worst.

Importantly, dehumanization through lack of substantial access to technology is not often due to malintent. On the grandest scale, no one is intentionally excluding people who lack access to a smartphone and the other things mentioned. Instead, structural expectations for a person to have such access display an active absence of concern for those who lack this access. At the same time, intent (or lack thereof) does not lessen the impact. Integral dehumanization does not require intent but rather the mechanism to be in place and spinning without anyone at the helm. This is the reason that it is the systems that must be dismantled; even people with the best of intentions cannot stop these systemic issues without actively dismantling these expectations and creating a replacement that allows for universal access that either eliminates the expectations all together or enables these expectations to be met.[42]

These three cases provide examples of how the Reign of God is obstructed by the reign of sin, obstructed by the common evil. In the spirit of Ellacuría's method, identifying these concrete problems that impact large segments of the population is essential in order to then move forward with steps to dismantle the obstruction. White supremacy, feminicide, and technology as an exclusionary force all serve to dehumanize vulnerable groups

---

42. As we will see in Chapter 4 below, the neoliberal response to this kind of question is to allow for the market to create solutions that make up for these access issues. The problem, however, is that the things we are discussing are not commodities that can be traded on the market. Instead, they are the very conditions to move beyond animal survival in our society. These technological elements are necessary conditions for human flourishing in our society, and they must be treated as more than mere commodities.

in society, obstructing God's love on a fundamental level. This prevents the realization of the Reign of God, which is the heart of Jesus's mission and the call to discipleship for his followers. In the face of these obstacles, our question must become "What must Christians do in response to this obstruction?"

Working toward the Reign of God: Defining a Humanizing Praxis

After considering the ways in which the common evil impacts our understanding of salvation in history and the enactment of Jesus's salvific work in history, we must look to how we can continue Christ's saving work in history. We can participate in Christ's salvific work only by working in love against the integral dehumanization of the common evil. We must, then, engage a humanizing praxis.

M. Shawn Copeland's theological work on solidarity is a valuable teacher for this work. By reflecting on the nature of solidarity and engaging Copeland's writing, we can begin to recognize how humanizing praxis lives at the heart of the realization of the Reign of God. Furthermore, attending to solidarity can heighten our awareness of what potential roadblocks like "white saviorism" are and, most importantly, how they can be avoided. As a cisgender, heterosexual-presenting white man, my writing and work can come from a well-intentioned desire to "save" the crucified people, using the power and privilege afforded me by the particularities of my birth as a force for liberation rather than oppression. Using my status in society and my complicity in my status, I can effectively other the crucified people as less-than-human precisely because of their crucifixion. While my intentions are good, the concrete actions they inspire can become yet another form of social dehumanization by collapsing their complex humanity into a one-dimensional infantilizing need to be saved by external actors.

A focus on solidarity, especially in the way that Copeland presents it, helps avoid such a social dehumanization. Solidarity is a joining-with that serves as the foundation for a new community in which we can experience the work of salvation together. As Sobrino writes in *Jesus the Liberator*, what Jesus asks of us in salvation is different for the oppressor and the oppressed.[43] For those of us holding the reigns of cultural power, salvation involves a conversion of the heart away from the oppressive structures that we have built and work to dismantle them in a spirit of atonement and love, not out of a desire to save. We are in need of salvation as well.

Solidarity, according to Copeland, is the response to suffering. The working definition of suffering Copeland offers is the one we will adopt here: "the disturbance of one's inner tranquility caused by physical, mental, emotional, and spiritual forces that are apprehended as jeopardizing one's very existence. Suffering, although not identical with evil, the negation and deprivation of some good, presses close to it."[44] Importantly for our project here, suffering, particularly unjust suffering, can be the result of the integral dehumanization that is the common evil. Our working definition of suffering, then, can be expanded with a few important distinctions. First, suffering can be the result of either natural necessity or historical necessity. Suffering brought about by natural necessity is part of the common human experience, providing an opportunity to find common ground and build the community we seek as social creatures. Suffering caused by historical necessity, or human actions, presses up against and connects to the common evil because it is a suffering that is unjust and, therefore, dehumanizing. The latter kind of suffering reveals the connec-

---

43. Jon Sobrino, *Jesus the Liberator* (Maryknoll, NY: Orbis Books, 1994), 96–97.

44. Copeland, *Knowing Christ Crucified*, 161.

tions between the reign of sin and the integral dehumanization of the common evil.

For Copeland, solidarity is the only response to suffering that does not continue dehumanization because it asks something of us. She moves us beyond a common misunderstanding of solidarity that is little more than meaningless connection, a sentiment that does not entail the praxis that is essential if we are to overcome the reign of sin. Solidarity must be something more because suffering demands a response from us. Solidarity cannot be reduced to easily spoken and even more easily forgotten platitudes.

Copeland defines solidarity as a form of discipleship through lived, compassionate action. This discipleship follows Christ's example of compassion, in which, according to the Gospels, Jesus is made sick to his stomach by the suffering he encountered.[45] This action must be both intelligent and effective. Its intelligence is driven by asking relevant questions; the action's effectiveness ensures that the action is not merely a waste of valuable time and resources. Such foundational criteria make solidaristic action that can actually impact the suffering of others in a positive manner without leading to unintended consequences that would in turn magnify the suffering of those one seeks to help.

Furthermore, solidarity is distinct from simply compassionate action in that solidarity seeks to address both the suffering in the moment and the systemic issues that give rise to widespread social suffering in the first place. There is nothing wrong with compassionate action. When you find someone severely hungry on the street, giving them something to eat is life-giving and good action. It is not solidarity, however, because it is an isolated act. Such an action can become solidaristic if it is put into a wider context that addresses hunger and its material causes.

---

45. Copeland, *Knowing Christ Crucified*, 174. Cf. Sobrino, *Jesus the Liberator*, 90–91.

This distinction between compassion and solidarity may seem counterintuitive, but our move with Copeland into a richer concept of solidarity requires concerted awareness of this different kind of praxis.

Copeland's understanding of solidarity is especially relevant to our conversation at this point: the compassionate acts of solidarity are inherently humanizing, pushing back against the common evil and the reign of sin that it represents. Framed within an integral humanization that seeks to realize the reign of God, Copeland's definition of solidarity provides an enriched understanding of a constitutive element of Christian discipleship and the vocation of the universal church.

The first element that must be considered is compassionate action as intelligent or well-thought-out. The intelligence behind compassionate action allows one to recognize the structural and material causes behind the dehumanization at work. Sometimes this aspect of solidaristic work can seem abstract, taking time away from action that would address the material concerns of those suffering. While this instinct has a point and feeding the hungry is an appropriate work of mercy, discreet acts of mercy cannot come at the expense of addressing the wider problem of why there are hungry people to begin with. Without reflection on the sinful social structures that cause people to go hungry, there will continue to be people who go hungry. In good medicine, one does not treat a bacterial infection with just pain relievers; the infection must also be treated with appropriate antibiotics. Otherwise, the patient will face the possibility of septic infection and death. Multifaceted, holistic consideration of a presenting infection is needed, and that includes addressing the structural issues that are present as well as alleviating the immediate suffering.

The first step in this kind of analysis is an act of epistemic humility, which discipleship requires. It is impossible to know everything; specialized knowledge is a major factor in how an interdependent society works. My knowledge as a scholar and a teacher of theology complements that of the carpenters, plumbers, lawyers, and countless other experts that make up our society. Any expert's knowledge has limits, and to pretend otherwise is a fool's errand. This means that different experts must be consulted regarding the different structural problems so that the proper conceptual framework can be used. Taking the example of widespread hunger, we see that expertise in economics, infrastructure, international trade, and agriculture is required to answer relevant questions of how vital goods like nutritious food and clean drinking water are so poorly distributed. Solidarity must be a collaborative effort, pulling both material and immaterial resources to perform compassionate actions that address both immediate and structural causes of suffering.

Another aspect of this humility actively seeks the contribution and insight of those who are suffering. One of the problems associated with the "white savior" attitude discussed above is that there is always a perception of what a suffering person or community needs is external to that person or community. This perception may not match the lived experience of that person or community, or, even worse, the perceived solution could unintentionally worsen the situation. It is essential, then, to ensure that the analysis of a situation includes the input of those in the midst of the situation. Without asking the question, "What can I do to help you?" we are not engaging the living realities of those who are suffering. Their suffering then becomes abstract, robbing it of both its immediacy and affective impact.

With the input of both experts in respective fields and the people whose suffering one is seeking to alleviate, a communal effort can begin planning an effective response. Looking to ensure that both immediate circumstances and structural causes of suffering are dealt with, such planning must be multifaceted, detailed, logical, and actionable. One of the major issues that some may find with this tact is the time that is required to build and implement such a plan. This is why compassionate action on a small scale is still necessary; people will starve waiting for a plan to come together that meets what is admittedly a high standard. Charitable and compassionate action should not and cannot stop while planning takes place. Once again, such action is necessary work, but it must be accomplished in conjunction with a larger project.

How does thinking about and planning for structural change humanize? Do these small acts of compassion, such as offering a meal to a hungry person on the street, not humanize?

Because the common evil is an *integral* dehumanization that must be addressed, we must seek a humanizing response that is effectively integral itself. In the example of hunger, the moment of sincere connection when someone who is suffering is offered a small comfort and short respite can be humanizing, but that short moment does not address the socially and psychologically dehumanizing circumstances that arise from food insecurity. The reign of sin impacts people in an integral fashion, integrating the evils of dehumanization into a complex of evil, and our praxis must respond by integrating the goods that contribute to the flourishing of the whole human person. We must constantly interrogate our goals and methods to ensure that all aspects of the person are addressed and respected. When we recognize and respect the inherent dignity of the human person in all of its complexity, we can participate in salvific integral humanization.

After constructing an intelligent plan of compassionate action, we must address the effectiveness of that plan. Building on the intelligence of compassionate actions, we must practice prudential judgment as we evaluate whether a plan will be effective or not.[46] This evaluative element is important for three reasons: it

---

46. Following Copeland, I am alluding to Lonergan's transcendental precepts: Be attentive, be intelligent, be reasonable, be responsible. This element

tests the intelligence of proposed action to verify the details of the sinful social structures at work; it ensures there is not a waste of resources on ineffective actions; and it opens another opportunity to bring those affected into the conversation regarding the intended results.

Analyzing the premises that go into the plan of action helpfully focuses action on the root of the problem. If a structure is incorrectly identified as the root of the problem, then the plan becomes a waste of time and resources. Part of this could come into the question of whether the experts who were consulted on the project were properly understood. Innocent misunderstanding can lead to disastrous consequences when planning like this is involved. Another question could be to consider what biases an expert may have had. For example, an economist trained in a particular school of economics may be wary of critiquing the free market when it could be a contributing factor in structural sin, especially when the maldistribution of vital goods is involved. Finally, one must ask the question of whether the proposed actions can even be accomplished with the resources available.

This last question feeds into a second concern regarding evaluating a plan: the use and misuse of resources. Actions that attempt to deal with systemic issues are by no means cheap and easy. Beyond the planning already discussed, these plans require resources of various kinds in order to happen at all. They require funding, political capital, hours of effort by a community willing to help, and general goodwill. These resources can be very difficult to reacquire if squandered, especially the intangibles. If a community sees the result of their labor as something that is fruitless and impotent, then the community will be less likely to

---

particularly addresses the third precept and its corresponding level of consciousness: judgment. For more on Lonergan's transcendental precepts, see Bernard Lonergan, "Method," in *Collected Works of Bernard Lonergan, Vol. 14: Method in Theology* (Toronto: University of Toronto Press, 2017), 20–27.

continue their efforts. Clear expectations and attainable goals are essential for this kind of group action in part because they prudently conserve resources for later use. Instead of snuffing out the flame of righteous indignation and calls for justice, this pragmatism recognizes the limits of one's actions so that the effort can be used in an appropriate manner.

The final piece from Copeland's understanding of solidarity that must be considered is the cost. This kind of discipleship expects something of us. For Copeland, solidarity discipleship entails a self-dispossession: engaging in *kenotic* action. Developing this further, she writes:

> Self-dispossession (*kenosis*) calls for the critique of autonomy as will-to-power, of obscurant individualism, of irresponsibility; but we must go further, deeper, beyond the boundaries of our lives/ourselves to a new way of being in the universe, in God's future. Dispossession of self implies the absolute surrender to God of all our cultural and social and religious and personal securities, the purification of our hearts and memories, the reorientation of ego, forgiveness.[47]

In its fullness, this cost is an entire transformation of our person into one who cannot only think of oneself. Solidarity is a call to a conversion of the heart that echoes the call of discipleship for people to "deny themselves and pick up their cross and follow me" (Matthew 16:24). Solidarity cannot leave one unchanged.

By renewing ourselves in the image of the ministry of Jesus of Nazareth, we are forever changed, and this renewing change allows us to be moved to compassionate action. Solidarity is a praxis-oriented conversion that leads to humanizing action. It is a necessary condition for the realization of the Reign of God. Perhaps solidarity is best understood as a transformative pro-

---

47. Copeland, *Knowing Christ Crucified*, 146.

cess in which compassionate action changes both the circumstance of the one who is suffering and the compassionate actor herself. Without this humanizing, compassionate action, the obstruction of the reign of sin will continue indefinitely.

Solidarity is made possible through the collaborative grace of God. Collaborative grace is a gift that allows us to overcome our selfishness and shortsightedness to engage in solidarity's thoughtful and compassionate action. Collaborative grace, as I recognize it, emerges from Doran's understanding of social grace and brings it to the level of praxis.

In *The Trinity and History, Volume I: Missions and Processions*, Doran describes social grace as the gift of the Holy Spirit that engages the entire scale of values. He writes:

> The integral functioning of the scale of values thus may be regarded as a social embodiment or objectification of the grace that is the communication of the grace that is the communication of divine life to men and women in the gift of the Holy Spirit, a communication that moves from above downward not only in human consciousness but also in the social objectification of that consciousness in the scale of values.[48]

The Holy Spirit, then, infuses the scale of values with the love that allows for conversion's transformative healing to take place, making healing action possible. In *The Trinity and History, Volume II: Missions, Relations, and Persons*, Doran expands on this, explaining that social grace is, at its core, about elevating human relations, communication, and collaboration to the imitation of love within the Godhead. Further, Doran argues that social grace is a contemporary way of discussing the Kingdom

---

48. Robert M. Doran, *The Trinity in History, Volume I: Missions and Processions* (Toronto: University of Toronto Press, 2012), 92.

of God.[49] Social grace demands constitutive meaning that is elaborated and revealed through collaboratively working with the invisible mission of the divine Word. Transposed onto the framework of integral human needs, social grace makes it possible for one to see through our biases and recognize the fullness of the inherent human dignity of our neighbors. The constitutive meaning that is demanded by social grace requires us to look the suffering other in the eye and acknowledge their humanity as well as the indignity of their suffering. Such recognition is transformative as it elaborates on the constitutive meaning, illuminating the injustice of a situation and the judgment that something must be done. This transformation then pushes us to act, driving us to engage in works that recognize said dignity and humanize those marginalized by society.

I refer to these practical manifestations of social grace as collaborative grace. Collaborative grace allows each of us to actively partake in the integral humanization of Jesus's salvific mission. Collaborative grace empowers us to take Jesus's outstretched hand and take our place to realize the Reign of God through humanizing solidarity amid the reign of sin. In collaborative grace, we can embody and pass on God's kenotic love to others who have been beaten down by the cruelties of a dehumanizing world and culture. Solidarity is made possible by collaborative grace, which empowers compassionate action to live a life of discipleship, as Copeland puts it, at the disposal of the cross.

Conclusion

Solidarity, grounded in collaborative grace, provides an opportunity to push back against and resist the obstructions to the Reign of God that are placed before us by the various forms of

---

49. Robert M. Doran, *The Trinity in History, Volume II: Missions, Relations, and Persons* (Toronto: University of Toronto Press, 2019), 28, 56–57.

structural dehumanization that are at work in the world. This is not an easy practice. The work is difficult, requiring both effort and skill to accomplish. Yet, this is the task to which we are called as Christians: to love one another through our actions, paying particular attention to the needs of the crucified peoples. Just as Jesus's mission was one of religious action that necessarily engaged the political realities of his day, our actions must engage with the sociopolitical structures that face us today, including political economies in the civilization of wealth that insist on our inhumanity.

3

A Political Theology of Dissent: Politico-Economic Impacts

> Justice worketh only within the bonds of things as they are ... and therefore though Justice is itself good and desireth no further evil, it can but perpetuate the evil that was, and doth not prevent it from the bearing of fruit in sorrow.
>
> J. R. R. Tolkien, *Morgoth's Ring*

Integral dehumanization has a wide range of impacts, but none are as apparent as the impacts in one's social context. So that we can fully understand the concrete and particular nature of the common evil, this chapter highlights both the political and economic impacts of integral dehumanization. By doing so, we can construct an appropriate and meaningful response: a political theology of dissent.

This chapter sets the stage for a political theology that can adequately engage the question of the political and economic impacts of the common evil. A discussion of the civilization of wealth and the civilization of poverty helpfully guides our approach to the politico-economic impacts of the common evil. Within this frame, patterns of integral dehumanization emerge. I highlight these patterns as they impact both the political and the economic elements of the human person. Finally, I argue for a political theology of dissent, thoroughly engaging questions of integral dehumanization.

The Civilizations of Wealth and Poverty

For Ellacuría, a liberation theology that grows from the tension between utopia and prophecy outlines a new human being that is "at once contemplative and active, one who transcends both leisure and business."[1] This human being embodies the necessary tension between theory and praxis, which shows that each is insufficient by itself; the human person must both hear and act out the Word of God. The human person engages the Word of God by both paying attention to the concrete reality in which she is active and accomplishing what is offered as promise.[2] In short, the human person whom Ellacuría's liberation theology outlines is one who, working to realize the Reign of God, follows the historical mission of Jesus of Nazareth.

This new human person, working to realize the Reign of God in cooperation with Jesus's mission, partakes in the creation of a new earth, which implies a new economic order that follows the utopian ideal.[3] Reading a passage from Marx's "A Contribution to the Critique of Hegel's Philosophy of Right" in light of a utopian-prophetic liberation theology, Ellacuría offers the following insight:

> The utopian ideal, when it is presented historically as gradually realizable and is assumed by the mass of the people, comes to be a stronger force than the force of arms; it is at once a material and a spiritual force, present and future,

---

1. Ignacio Ellacuría, "Utopia and Propheticism from Latin America: A Concrete Essay in Historical Soteriology," in J. Matthew Ashley, Kevin F. Burke, S.J., and Rodolfo Cardenal, S.J., eds., *A Grammar of Justice: The Legacy of Ignacio Ellacuría* (Maryknoll, NY: Orbis Books, 2014), 38.
2. Ellacuría, "Utopia and Propheticism," 38.
3. Ellacuría, "Utopia and Propheticism," 38–39.

A Political Theology of Dissent

hence able to overcome the material-spiritual complexity with which the course of history presents itself.[4]

Here, Ellacuría emphasizes that the utopian ideal, backed with the momentum of the masses, can overcome any "complexity" that it may encounter. This "complexity" is the ideological tension that is created by the friction of two discordant ideas. One example is the friction between the utopian concept of true equality for all people in the Reign of God and the construct of meritocracy that free-market capitalism values. Capitalist ideology creates a framework in which one is told that hard work allows one to attain one's heart's desires; implicit in this claim is the assumption that those whose basic needs are not satisfied have not worked hard enough. Friction, and therefore tension, is created when this kind of cultural ideologization runs up against the gospel's message of inherent human dignity and the moral imperative to ensure basic needs are satisfied. This tension is overcome by the momentum of the masses. In terms of economic order, the utopian ideal calls for the replacement of the current economic order—the civilization of wealth and of capital—with a civilization of poverty and of work.[5]

---

4. Ellacuría, "Utopia and Propheticism," 39.

5. Ellacuría, "Utopia and Propheticism," 39. Sobrino offers some brief and helpful clarification here. While most of the commentators in *A Grammar of Justice* refer only to the civilization of wealth, Sobrino reinforces the link to capital. In reference to Ellacuría's "The Challenge of the Poor Majority," Sobrino claims Ellacuría understood the civilization of wealth and the civilization of capital as the same concept. While the connection to capital is important, I will use the term civilization of wealth to maintain continuity with my interlocutors. For more on Sobrino's reading, see Jon Sobrino, "*Extra Pauperes Nulla Salus*: A Short Utopian-Prophetic Essay," in *No Salvation Outside the Poor: Prophetic-Utopian Essays* (Maryknoll, NY: Orbis Books, 2008), 35–76.

The Civilization of Wealth and of Capital

Ellacuría describes the civilization of wealth as a system that understands the foundation of society as the private accumulation of the maximum amount of capital on the part of a unit, whether it be an individual, family, corporation, or state. The private accumulation of capital grounds concepts of development, security, and consumption thought to be necessary for happiness in this society. Furthermore, Ellacuría, referencing state capitalism in the East, shows how the civilization of wealth transcends the Western democracy/Soviet communism dialectic.[6] The acquisition and accumulation of capital are not strictly Western phenomena. While the civilization of wealth has brought about benefits for humanity that must be preserved, the evils it has brought about are more devastating and cannot be self-corrected.[7]

The evils brought about by the civilization of wealth fall into three primary categories: capital as the fundamental basis of development, the failure to meet basic needs, and the dehumanization of the poor. Focusing on these three categories helps to clarify and concretize Ellacuría's critique of the civilization of wealth.

The first category of evils is capital as the fundamental basis of development. This category ties together the economic issues at hand with the civilization of wealth and the question of colo-

---

6. Ellacuría, "Utopia and Propheticism," 40. It is worth noting that according to the editors of *A Grammar of Justice*, Ellacuría wrote this essay in 1989. The Berlin Wall fell on November 9, 1989, a week to the day before Ellacuría was martyred. While this may be speculation, it appears that Ellacuría thought the communism represented by the USSR would inevitably fail, leading to a spread of capitalism that would make the capitalist iteration of the civilization of wealth a global standard. This spread has resulted in the phenomenon of globalization, making Ellacuría's critique relevant thirty years later.

7. Ellacuría, "Utopia and Propheticism," 40.

nialization that is ever present in Latin America. In his lecture "Latin American Quincentenary: Discovery or Cover-up?" Ellacuría develops this concept in the language of the civilization of capital and the civilization of work. The following excerpt provides a very clear outline of the relationships between development and the civilization of capital:

> The important thing is that the destiny of humanity not be controlled by the internal laws of capital. Because these laws, though not immoral, are amoral; and they follow a certain dynamic that pulls along everyone involved in it. We can say that capitalists do not create capital, but capital creates capitalists and pushes them to do what they are doing in the West and also in the Soviet Union. Because the defining issue is not the possession of capital in private or in collective hands. That is an important point to distinguish, but it is not the fundamental issue. Fundamentally, they are both civilizations of capital. And we all know that in its very development, capital does many things that are not only useless and deceptive to humanity but that also oblige most of humanity to live in a certain way, in a problematic way.[8]

The dynamic of the amoral laws of capitalism is an engine that pulls all involved in a singular direction: toward the accumulation of capital. This pull leads humanity to live in a problematic way that opens the door to the occasion of sin and oppression. Put concretely, the reality of capital drives a desire to accumulate it in a way that may be legal if not moral, regardless of who owns the capital.

According to Ellacuría, both Western nations, particularly

---

8. Ignacio Ellacuría, "Latin American Quincentenary: Discovery or Cover-up?" in *Essays on History, Liberation, and Salvation* (Maryknoll, NY: Orbis Books, 2013), 27–38, 35.

the United States, and Eastern nations, such as the Soviet Union, live in ways that are defined by capital. The occasion of sin and oppression set the stage for even "development" itself to be defined by capital. The definition of a "developed" nation is formed by understanding the relationship between a nation's culture and capital.

Following this formula, the two superpowers in Ellacuría's day, the United States and the Soviet Union, were considered the most developed nations, while a nation such as El Salvador, which had a culture that was not defined by capital, was less developed. In the midst of the Cold War, each superpower sought to extend its influence into other nations, leading to what Ellacuría would call the same effect: the "development" of these nations and their cultures into models of the civilization of capital that entail a problematic way of living. Ellacuría is quick to point out that the U.S. solution that was offered to El Salvador's problems was a bad solution; that is, the solution was worse than the very problems it purported to address.[9] Instead of actually solving the problems of the Salvadoran people, it compounded their suffering with a new problematic way of living.

The next category of evils is one aspect of this problematic way of living: the failure to meet basic needs. This is a concrete example of the common evil. When basic necessities such as nutritious food, clean drinking water, housing, primary education, sufficient employment, and basic health care fail to be met, members of the community suffer.[10] A common way that this occurs is through the maldistribution of vital goods, the goods by which basic needs are met.[11] According to the logic of the civi-

---

9. Ellacuría, "Latin American Quincentenary," 34.
10. Ellacuría, "Utopia and Propheticism," 41.
11. The language of the maldistribution of vital goods is not from Ellacuría but a phrase from Robert Doran's *Theology and the Dialectics of History* (Toronto: University of Toronto Press, 1991). Doran's language helps to

lization of wealth, the accumulation of the greatest amount of capital leads to the acquisition of goods. In this logic, one can infer that the improper distribution of vital goods is related to the wealthy accumulating these goods beyond their needs, leaving the poor majorities without adequate resources of their own.

This maldistribution of vital goods has a material dimension and a systemic dimension. The material dimension deals with the hording of material goods, such as clean drinking water. Clean drinking water can sometimes be difficult to find in communities where pollution from manufacturing or another source runs unchecked and makes it a scarce resource. When a resource becomes scarce, its value increases, which makes it likely to be acquired by those with sufficient capital to do so. In the civilization of wealth, one who has invested capital into a commodity—in this case clean drinking water—expects to make a profit on their investment. This means that clean drinking water will be sold at a certain percentage above cost, which makes it difficult for those who lack financial resources to obtain sufficient amounts of water. Simply put, the civilization of wealth is designed to prey on those who live below a certain financial threshold. This dimension of the maldistribution of vital goods has a direct and clear impact on the material conditions of the poor majority—in Ellacuría's Latin America and elsewhere—by limiting their access to a basic necessity of life, thus entailing suffering.

The systemic dimension of the maldistribution of vital goods is highlighted by the privation of structural goods, namely, primary education and sufficient employment. In the civilization of wealth, there is an expectation that adult members will engage in common projects and work. This engagement requires a basic set of skills and a means of applying those skills. Primary edu-

---

clarify the structural elements of Ellacuría's concerns with the civilization of wealth and makes my argument here clearer.

cation and sufficient employment provide both this set of skills and the means of applying them and allow for one to be fully part of the community.

When these structural vital goods are not widely available, there is a twofold impact. First, these structural goods become scarce and are turned into commodities in the same way as the material goods described above. When education and employment become commodities, those without sufficient financial means are left with incomplete educations and jobs that do not provide enough compensation to survive, let alone fully engage in society. Second, those who are deprived of primary education and sufficient employment are marginalized by society, which leaves them even more isolated and vulnerable to exploitation. These examples of situational poverty become generational poverty, where the condition of parents is continued among their children and their children's children, and so on, making the inequality a persistent problem.[12] Without the means or the ability to break the cycle of poverty, the poor become an underclass of society, ignored by the wealthy minority and denied the basic necessities for a dignified life.

Exploitation leads to the final category of evils brought upon by the civilization of wealth: the dehumanization of the

---

12. In the context of the United States, this set of circumstances was usually dismissed due to upward social mobility, the phenomenon where a person is able to enter through thrift and enterprise a higher socioeconomic class than the one into which she was born. Social mobility, however, is not as common as it once was. According to a 2019 report from the Stanford Center on Poverty and Inequality, social mobility has been on a steady decline since the 1980s, which is when neoliberal politico-economic policies were put in place by the Reagan administration. The report also cites that millennials, individuals born between 1980 and 1996, are likely the first generation to experience more downward social mobility than upward social mobility. For more, see Michael Hout, *State of the Union: Social Mobility* (Stanford, CA: Stanford Center on Poverty and Inequality, 2019), https://inequality.stanford.edu/sites/default/files/Pathways_SOTU_2019_SocialMobility.pdf.

poor.¹³ Ellacuría says very little explicitly about the question of dehumanization in relation to the civilization of wealth, but he does offer an implicit commentary based on positive statements that he makes regarding John Paul II's *Laborem exercens*. In Ellacuría's integration of *Laborem exercens* with the demands of liberation theology, he distinguishes between a humanist materialism and an economic materialism.

Humanist materialism recognizes the complexity of the material conditions of the human person and avoids idealistic solutions to the real problems that people encounter. Economic materialism, however, does not take the material complexity of human reality into consideration. This failure, in turn, leads to idealistic solutions to human problems that are practically untenable.¹⁴

The U.S. capitalist adage "To pull yourself up by your own bootstraps" provides a concrete example of one of these idealistic failings. With enough grit and fiscal self-discipline, a person is supposed to be able to work her way out of any dire socioeconomic situation. This fits Ellacuría's implied description, insofar as it is idealistic and ignores the complex reality that a human person experiences.

To demonstrate this idealism, consider the hypothetical case of Amy. Amy lives in Milwaukee, Wisconsin. Wisconsin follows the federal minimum wage, which is $7.25 per hour. For her forty-hour-per-week job that pays the federal minimum wage, her weekly wage, prior to tax withholdings, is $290, or an

---

13. Jon Sobrino, in *"Extra Pauperes Nulla Sallus,"* offers a long discussion of dehumanization in relation to contemporary issues of globalization. This essay, among others by Sobrino, will be a helpful commentary throughout this chapter and will be discussed in relation to capitalist responses to questions of inequality. For the full essay, see Jon Sobrino, *"Extra Pauperes Nulla Sallus,"* 35–76.

14. Ellacuría, "Utopia and Propheticism," 40.

annual gross salary of $15,080.[15] According to the University of Wisconsin-Milwaukee, a person who lives alone can expect to spend $785 per month on rent for a studio apartment in the Milwaukee area, excluding utilities.[16] At roughly $9,420 a year, Amy's rent alone would take up 62 percent of her income, leaving her with $5,660 of her annual income to cover the rest of her needs. If we assume that she spends only $60 per week for groceries, Amy would spend $3,120 annually on food. Amy would be able to participate in the state of Wisconsin's BadgerCare Plus program, a low-income health insurance program, because her annual income is less than 100% of the Federal Poverty Line.[17] Without a healthcare insurance premium, Amy would have $2,540 annually, or $211.67 per month, to pay for any utilities that are not covered by her rent, her clothing needs, her transportation costs, and other miscellaneous expenses the average adult incurs. Given that utilities and transportation costs will take up a significant portion of Amy's remaining wages, there is very little in the way of available funds to save. Amy would likely be able to avail herself of the protections of the social safety net, but this lack of self-reliance runs contrary to the ideal solution. The civilization of wealth's proposed solution prioritizes hard work, thrift, and saving as the only necessary factors to escape financial hardship. This solution is idealistic in a detrimental way.

The idealistic solution reduces human struggle into variables in an equation that should balance once all factors are taken

---

15. For the sake of simplicity of this example, we will not factor in tax withholdings.

16. See, "Finances," University of Wisconsin-Milwaukee Off-Campus Resource Center, uwm.edu/off-campus-resources/finances/.

17. For more information on the BadgerCare Plus program's income limit and extensions threshold, see https://www.dhs.wisconsin.gov/badgercareplus/fpl.htm. As of the time of publication, the dollar amounts were effective February 1, 2025 to January 31, 2026. Note that the dollar amounts in the BadgerCare Plus program may change as the Federal Poverty Line data changes.

A Political Theology of Dissent

into consideration. The idealistic solution cannot recognize the possibility that ends might not meet, even if Amy does everything she is "supposed to do" to fulfill the ideal. Should Amy encounter any of the real problems that people face—getting sick, having emergency expenses, and even losing one's employment through layoffs—she can no longer succeed because these setbacks are not taken into account by the idealistic solution.

By constructing an answer that ignores these very real and very basic aspects of human life, the civilization of wealth disregards the human experience and dehumanizes the person. Amy becomes an operation among variables in the economic equation. Her struggles are viewed as irrelevant, and her concerns go unnoticed. This dehumanized person is expected to perform the operations as set forth by the equation or be considered a failure.

Jon Sobrino adds to this analysis by emphasizing how the idealistic solutions to the poverty of the late twentieth and early twenty-first centuries further this dehumanization. He writes:

> The first dehumanizing aspect of the attempts to eliminate poverty is the way they effectively bracket people's dignity, as if it were a matter of principle, as if one thing had nothing to do with the other. It is simply accepted that any means is good as long as it alleviates poverty. This way of thinking is not only unethical, but it is dehumanizing, for we are not talking about feeding a species of wild animal, but about nourishing human beings.[18]

Sobrino highlights the dehumanizing aspect of the sterile, mathematical approach to "solving" the problem of poverty. Attempts to solve problems related to poverty—namely inflation and the impact that it has on wages and unemployment—approach poverty as a matter of finding the right variables to

---

18. Sobrino, "*Extra Pauperes Nulla Salus*," 41.

balance equations. Ellacuría and Sobrino both acknowledge that our lived historical reality as human beings is never so simple that it can be adequately reduced to such variables.

One could argue that these concerns about dehumanization are merely emotional responses to the hard facts of what must be done to ensure economic and civic well-being. While this underdeveloped understanding of human dignity is not entirely incorrect regarding freedom of choice, the application of choice in this concrete example tends to undercut the same human dignity that it claims to support. Sobrino argues that this supposed emotional response is actually an ethics concern. When this concern for the ethical is divorced from praxis and policy, says Sobrino, only cold-hearted pragmatism and a strong potential for brutality remain.[19] In this way, Sobrino echoes Ellacuría's point that materialist economism is not ethical in its own internal dynamism and its effects.[20]

In addition to recognizing the complexities of the material conditions of human reality, materialist humanism offers a second element for maintaining the human person as subject in economic relations: "This materialist humanism aims to overcome materialist economism, since it would no longer be economic matter that finally determines everything else, as is the case in any type of civilization of capital and wealth, but human material complex and open, which conceives human beings as the limited but real subjects of their own history."[21] Under economic materialism, the human person is reduced to an object, for, at its core, economic materialism is based on instrumental thinking. Under humanist materialism, the human person is a real subject of their own history.

---

19. Sobrino, "*Extra Pauperes Nulla Salus*," 42.
20. Ellacuría, "Utopia and Propheticism," 40.
21. Ellacuría, "Utopia and Propheticism," 40.

In the case of economic materialism, the human being is reduced to a tool and, therefore, objectified and dehumanized. As tools are efficient at their task—a wrench that can provide optimal leverage to secure a bolt is good but a ratchet with a perfectly fitting socket would be better—the objectified human being becomes a tool that exists only to maximize profit through the most efficient means possible. Amy is the means to the accumulation of capital. Again, her human needs—material, intellectual, emotional, and spiritual—are irrelevant to driving the economic engine forward so long as they do not cost the engine too much profit. The economy and the wealthy few who direct its force treat Amy, and each of her fellow laborers, as if she were a replaceable cog that is useful only so long as she keeps the machine running efficiently.

Pressured by the need for more income to break even, Amy is forced to take on a part-time job, working an additional twenty hours per week for the same minimum wage. This raises her pretax income by 50 percent to $22,620. This also means that Amy is working sixty hours as opposed to forty hours per week, and she is likely working every day of the week. These sixty hours also do not include her commute time and the unpaid lunch breaks during her shifts. This burdensome work schedule means that Amy likely has little time and money with which to socialize with friends, pursue hobbies, and engage in other activities that maintain a healthy sense of self. This leads Amy and others in similar situations to internalize the dehumanizing vision of themselves held by those whose concern extends only as far as the economy remains profitable.

Amy's situation as described here is an example of the economic dehumanization discussed briefly above. The economic-materialist perspective creates a situation in which Amy is integrally dehumanized; she is deprived both of the basic physical necessities for survival and of the social, psychological, spiritual, and intellectual needs that allow for a truly human life. The materialist economic worldview that characterizes the civilization of wealth transforms people, including the wealthy themselves at times, into economic units to be manipulated in the wider search for profit.

The three evils of the civilization of wealth described above provide a groundwork for a culture in which the production of wealth and capital are the engine of cultural progress. The change in definition of development, maldistribution of vital goods, and dehumanization of the poor show how the civilization of capital creates an unjust society that is both unethical and contrary to a salvific praxis of the Reign of God. The combination of these three evils creates the second aspect of our wider concern: political dehumanization. In this context, I am using political in terms of the well-being of society. An unhealthy and inhumane society happens when human beings are dehumanized so that the wider society can function, or, worse, flourish, only in a selective way. When human beings, the bedrock and telos of society, are thrown to the wayside for the sake of society's supposed well-being, something has gone wrong on a fundamental level. The civilization of wealth exemplifies this tremendous failing.

The Civilization of Poverty and of Work

Prophetic-utopian thought, as Ellacuría highlights, proposes a better solution: the civilization of poverty. The civilization of poverty and of work is named this way to show its contrast to the civilization of wealth and of capital, not to glorify the dehumanizing poverty that is sin.[22] For this project, the civiliza-

---

22. One way in which Ellacuría's civilization of poverty could be interpreted in a positive light is in the spiritual poverty described by the Latin American Bishops Conference document from the Medellín Conference in 1968, specifically "Poverty of the Church," September 6, 1968.

tion of poverty is the different dynamism that is needed in order to salvifically overcome wealth and capital.[23] Following Ellacuría, questions of society and, by extension, of political economy must be answered in terms of salvation. Sobrino points out that Ellacuría means that salvation takes shape through the satisfaction of basic needs, with the dignity of the human person, in freedom from oppression, by coming together as family rather than merely a species, and through other concrete articulations.[24] While Sobrino is correct on this point, I think that recalling Ellacuría's task of taking charge of the weight of reality is a better way to express the salvific opportunity. In taking charge of the weight of reality, we make a concerted effort to engage in the collaborative project of realizing the Reign of God that is at hand. In this collaborative effort, Sobrino describes forms of salvation that are integrated into the larger soteriological and eschatological picture that Ellacuría envisions.

The three major elements of the civilization of poverty that are relevant to our discussion of a theologically informed political economy are the primacy of the satisfaction of basic needs, the dignifying of work and the worker, and the increase in shared solidarity. Each element has a salvific quality that we must explore as we embrace salvific dynamism. Together, these three elements provide a clearer understanding of a society that is oriented toward salvation and justice.

First, the satisfaction of basic needs serves as a counterpoint to *el mal común* of the civilization of wealth. The civilization of poverty accomplishes the satisfaction of basic needs by creating "an economic arrangement that relies on and directly and immediately addresses the satisfaction of basic needs of all humans."[25] Ellacuría is very open-ended in how one is to define

---

23. Ellacuría, "Utopia and Propheticism," 41.
24. Sobrino, *"Extra Pauperes Nulla Salus,"* 57.
25. Ellacuría, "Utopia and Propheticism," 41.

basic needs, allowing for cultural and individual particularities. Ultimately, one must look to the reality of extreme poverty to provide a unifying framework for these basic needs. Ellacuría offers an initial list of basic needs, namely, proper nutrition, clean drinking water, housing, health care, primary education, and sufficient employment. He also admits that this is just a starting point, for the list can be expanded as needed to address a particular context.[26] As we covered in the previous chapter, sufficient internet access and the skills necessary to use it are important additions to this list in the U.S. context.[27]

Freedom from domination is foundational for the salvific satisfaction of basic needs. Remember that liberation is, in part, a transformation of the historical. The historical implies the pre-existence of a material reality that can be changed. Therefore, when one transforms the historical by ensuring that the basic needs of all persons are satisfied, one is collaboratively working to realize the Reign of God.

Second, the dignifying and humanizing effect of work is a powerful counterpoint to the civilization of wealth. Work is intended to perfect the human person.[28] In Ellacuría's context, the term *trabajo* is a common word for work or job.[29] Ellacuría goes beyond the common usage of the term, drawing from John

---

26. Ellacuría, "Utopia and Propheticism," 41.
27. It is worth noting another important addition to Ellacuría's list in the context of the United States: universal health care. There are several arguments that conclude that given Catholic social teaching's emphasis on a guarantee of adequate health care for all, universal health care in the United States is essential. For an example of this form of argumentation rooted in solidarity, see Agnus Sibley, "Health Care's Ills: A Catholic Diagnosis," *Linacre Quarterly* 83, no. 4 (2016): 402–22.
28. Ellacuría, "Utopia and Propheticism," 41.
29. All references to the Spanish text are found in Ignacio Ellacuría, "Utopía y profetismo desde América Latina. Un ensayo concreto de soteriología histórica," in *Escritos teológicos, II* (San Salvador: UCA Editores, 2000), 233–94.

Paul II's encyclical *Laborem exercens*.[30] Specifically, Ellacuría focuses our attention on what John Paul II called work in the subjective sense. While reflecting on the connection to Genesis 1 and the divine command to "subdue the earth," John Paul II argues the following:

> Man has to subdue the earth and dominate it, because as the "image of God" he is a person, that is to say, a subjective being capable of acting in a planned and rational way, capable of deciding about himself, and with a tendency to self-realization. As *a person, man is therefore the subject of work*. As a person, he performs various actions belonging to the work process; independently of their objective content, these actions must all serve to realize his humanity, to fulfill the calling to be a person that is his by reason of his very humanity.[31]

John Paul II places an emphasis on work as a way for the human person to become more fully human. Through work in the subjective sense, one can understand and fulfill one's vocation. "Work," then, must not be taken as a simple synonym for employment. One can be employed in a way that does not provide this same self-realization.[32] More importantly, the civilization of poverty seeks to provide all with work in this subjective sense. Work that allows for one to self-realize is inherently dignified, building a community that shares in this realization.

---

30. John Paul II, *Laborem exercens* (Vatican City: Liberia Editrice Vaticana, 1981).

31. *Laborem exercens*, §6 (emphasis in original).

32. This can be understood in two ways. First, there are jobs that are dehumanizing in the treatment of workers, dangerous working conditions, and lack of proper compensation. Second, there are jobs that seem to have no purpose beyond than putting a person behind a desk. Anthropologist David Graeber refers to the latter type of job as "bullshit jobs," which perform a form of spiritual violence upon the worker. For more, see David Graeber, *Bullshit Jobs: A Theory* (New York: Simon & Schuster, 2018).

Ellacuría frames this subjective sense of work in terms of humanization; humanizing work is a central aspect of building the civilization of poverty. Humanizing work stands in sharp contrast to the competitive, dehumanizing work of the civilization of capital. Ellacuría briefly describes work in the civilization of capital as consisting of exploitations of oneself and others that are rooted in inequalities, which, in turn, cause domination and antagonism. These issues are caused by the dynamics of capital that shape society in ways that place the accumulation of capital as the highest value. This highest value naturally breeds competition, which is the sign of a healthy economy and society within the free-market, capitalist point of view. The problem, however, is that this competition turns quite easily into an antagonism that alters the way people relate to one another. These alterations—namely, seeing other people as either enemies to be dominated or objects to be exploited—inevitably lead to one's exploitation of oneself; one is willing to sacrifice relationships and other noncommercial aspects of oneself for the sake of accumulating capital. Self-exploitation causes misery and isolation, for which the only remedy is the accumulation of more capital. At this point, a negative feedback loop occurs, restarting the cycle with a further desire to acquire capital. If a focal point of a society is the accumulation of capital, then Ellacuría's description naturally follows.

This dynamism of capital acquisition will naturally form a very different society than one formed by the dynamisms of humanizing work and the satisfaction of basic needs. According to Ellacuría, the dynamisms of the laws of capital, however, have begun to move the marginalized in the direction of creating a different society.[33] Importantly for Ellacuría, movement in the

---

33. Ellacuría, "Utopia and Propheticism," 41–42. In the contemporary United States, the shift is beginning to move in the direction of questioning capitalism, especially among younger Americans. According to a report in

direction of dynamisms of humanizing work is not enough. The community cannot simply escape the civilization of wealth and form a new society as a sign of protest. The community must engage and renew the world, transforming it "in the direction of the utopia of the new earth."[34] Put another way, engaging and transforming the civilization of capital is part of the salvific task of realizing the Reign of God and participating in the mission of Jesus of Nazareth. This transforming engagement takes charge of the weight of reality as the collaborative effort to change the direction of history in a way that is in line with what Jesus calls us to do.

Third, shared solidarity enacts the language of community as a central aspect of the civilization of poverty. Ellacuría's discussion of shared solidarity mirrors the critique of competition and antagonism discussed above, but he adds a central point of "the common enjoyment of common property."[35] At its core, Ellacuría understands common property as the rejection of any capitulation to the sin that drives us to consider private ownership driven by greed. He writes:

> When the church's social doctrine, following Saint Thomas, holds that private appropriation of goods is the

---

the *Washington Post* from April 2016, over half (51 percent) of survey respondents between 18 and 29 years of age to a Harvard University poll said they do not support capitalism. Given the stated margin of error of 2.4 percent and the representative study sample, this translates to anywhere between 48.6 percent and 53.4 percent of young adults in the United States do not support capitalism. This makes sense as Millennials and Generation Z, who made up the 18–29 age group for the survey, were significantly impacted by the fallout of the 2007–2008 financial crisis. For more details, see Max Ehrenfreund, "A majority of millennials now reject capitalism, poll shows," *Washington Post*, April 26, 2016, https://www.washingtonpost.com/news/wonk/wp/2016/04/26/a-majority-of-millennials-now-reject-capitalism-poll-shows/.

34. Ellacuría, "Utopia and Propheticism," 42.
35. Ellacuría, "Utopia and Propheticism," 42.

best practical manner for their primordial common destiny to be fulfilled in an orderly way, it is making a concession to "the hardness of their hearts," but "in the beginning it was not so." Only because of greed and selfishness, connatural to original sin, can it be said that private ownership of property is the best guarantee of productive advancement and social order. But if "where sin abounded, grace abounded more" is to have historical verification, it is necessary to proclaim in a utopian way that a new earth with new human beings must be shaped with principles of greater altruism and solidarity.[36]

The private accumulation of common property can easily be framed in contemporary terms by considering the topic of "privatization." Privatization need not only be contrasted with public ownership, as in the case of a public utility. It can also be contrasted with the idea that a common resource can be shared among members of the community without involving commercial exchange.

Ellacuría points us to "the benefits of nature." He names several natural features and discusses how they can be shared by a community for production, use, and enjoyment without any formal owner.[37] Consider Ellacuría's example of the seas.

---

36. Ellacuría, "Utopia and Propheticism," 42. While the editors of the text highlight the explicit scriptural references to Matthew 19:8 and Romans 5:20, there is another passage that underlies this idea. In Acts 4:32–37, the group of believers who are with the apostles forsook private ownership for the sake of communal ownership. As v. 34 puts clearly: "There was not a needy person among them."

37. Ellacuría, "Utopia and Propheticism," 43. This concept is difficult to explain fully in the contemporary American context because, quite simply, the vast majority of the land in the United States is owned by either an individual, a corporation, or a government, whether it be municipal, state, or federal. Even the Boston Common, the oldest public park in the United States, which had originated as common grazing fields, is technically owned by the City of Boston.

One can fish for sustenance, enjoy a swim, or travel by way of a seafaring vessel; none of these options requires the seas to be owned by an entity, whether a private individual or a state. Ellacuría envisions entering into relationship with others in a community and with creation itself.[38] If a body of water were to be owned by an entity, the options for use would be severely limited due to the expectation of exchange.[39]

The question of common property is part of what makes us truly human, offering an anthropological vision for the human person as communal. Continuing this line of thinking, Ellacuría writes:

> If a social order were achieved in which basic needs were satisfied in a stable manner and were guaranteed, and the common sources of personal development were made possible, so that the security and the possibilities of personal development were guaranteed, the present order based on the accumulation of private capital and material wealth could be considered as a prehistoric and pre-human stage. The utopian ideal is not that all are to have much by means

---

38. Ellacuría's understanding of the concept common property and its ecological dimension would be able to enter into dialogue with Pope Francis's encyclical *Laudato si'*, especially given each figure's concern for the poor. This connection goes beyond the limits of the current project, but it is a worthwhile topic for future research.

39. One way the issue of private ownership is argued is the question of responsibility. Ownership implies responsibility, which is inherently individualistic from the capitalist perspective. Given that assumption, the possibility of a shared communal space does not make sense; a community cannot have responsibility. A person can only be expected to be responsible for themselves and not for others, or so the line of capitalist thought argues. Following from those assumptions, the only way for a "common space" to be properly cared for is for an individual to be responsible for it; private ownership, therefore, is a necessity. In other words, it is a question of philosophical and theological anthropology that drives the issue at hand; can human beings be responsible without the impetus of self-interest?

of private and exclusive appropriation, but that all are to have what is necessary and that the non-acquisitive and nonexclusive use and enjoyment of what is primarily common be open to all. The indispensable dynamism of personal initiative cannot be confused with the natural-original dynamism of private and privatizing initiative. Nor is excluding others as competitors to one's selfhood the only way to work for oneself or to be oneself.[40]

The strength behind Ellacuría's point is that the utopian ideal offers a vision of the human person that does not frame human reality solely in the context of economic terms and relations. The virtues that are rightly associated with capitalism, such as personal initiative and freedom, are not exclusive to the framework of the civilization of wealth. Instead, the civilization of poverty allows these virtues, too, to integrate within a communal framework. This framework, shaped by common experience and projects, builds solidarity within the community and leaves no one to suffer alone.

Satisfying basic needs, humanizing work, and community-focused structure are integrated humanizations that undo the effects of the common evil. The satisfaction of basic needs provides for physical needs. Humanizing work contributes to one's psychological needs, allowing one to see the value their labor has on the world and stimulating one's curiosity in meaningful work. In a similar manner, the communal structure of the civilization of poverty fulfills the social needs. The intellectual and spiritual needs discussed above can be met on multiple levels: in the humanizing work that stirs and challenges the intellect; deep, reflective conversations with friends and loved ones; and in the bonds made within the churches and faith communities in which one finds oneself. This is key for understanding the

---

40. Ellacuría, "Utopia and Propheticism," 43.

stark difference between these two civilization frameworks: the civilization of wealth is integrally dehumanizing, pushing people to live less-than-human lives, while the civilization of poverty emphasizes human dignity and flourishing, integrally humanizing each member of the community.

The preceding discussion of the civilization of wealth and the civilization of poverty reveals the fruits of the utopian-prophetic framework. The prophetic critique highlights the violence of the civilization of wealth that dehumanizes and alienates members of a community from one another. The utopian ideal is sought through and labored for in the civilization of poverty, which elevates the dignity of the human being and works to realize the Reign of God.

The Economic Question of Unemployment

At this point, we can see the politico-economic impacts of the common evil as not only concerns for ethics but also for a systematic theology. Ellacuría explicitly connects questions of economics to questions of systematic theology, namely, sin, soteriology, and eschatology. In a brief article entitled "The Kingdom of God and Unemployment in the Third World," Ellacuría argues that unemployment is a theological problem and not only an economic one. In his argument, Ellacuría reveals that questions of economics, such as unemployment, can also be questions that concern both theological ethics and systematic theology.

Ellacuría begins the article by outlining the specific situation of unemployment in the Third World, citing it as a defining problem of the majority of the earth's population.[41] The problem

---

41. Ignacio Ellacuría, "The Kingdom of God and Unemployment in the Third World," *Concilium* 10 (1982): 91–96, 92. Ellacuría refers to unemployment in the First World as a marginal problem, which follows given the significant wealth disparity between the United States and Third World nations such as El Salvador. I would argue, however, that while Ellacuría's point still

of unemployment in the Third World is, according to Ellacuría, "massive and chronic and is bound up with the economic order."[42] Put another way, unemployment in that context is a systemic failure of the economic order that goes well beyond what one could consider an acceptable unemployment rate in a "healthy" economy.[43] Systemic failure means that unemployment is not just a fluke that will be corrected by the nature of the business cycle. This problem, Ellacuría points out, is due to the unequal footing between trade partners on the global scale, which leaves Third World nations at the mercy of First World nations, whose only concern is their own profitability and benefit. The First World can make economic demands of the Third World without concern for backlash, and the Third World suffers for it.[44]

Complementing the systemic problem is the lack of widespread relief in the form of a social safety net. When Ellacuría was writing, only 5 percent of workers in El Salvador were qualified for social security, leaving the vast majority of the population without any assistance to mitigate the effects of their poverty.[45] Both the state and the economy had failed the majority of the population.

People in rural communities and families with dependents, specifically children and young adults, were two populations

---

stands nearly forty years later, the situation in the United States has worsened due to policies that weaken the social safety net. Given this change, Ellacuría's argument has gained purchase in the context of the United States.

42. Ellacuría, "The Kingdom of God and Unemployment," 92.

43. A good unemployment rate is generally seen as any number below 5 percent. As Ellacuría mentions, the United States had an unemployment rate of 10 percent in 1982, which was the highest unemployment rate since World War II. The situation in the United States in 1982 is not, however, a sign of the systemic imbalance as seen in Third World countries during Ellacuría's lifetime. These numbers also do not reflect the problem of underemployment, which complicates the picture greatly.

44. Ellacuría, "The Kingdom of God and Unemployment," 92.

45. Ellacuría, "The Kingdom of God and Unemployment," 92.

that concerned Ellacuría in his work on unemployment. While those in the former category could live with few resources, unemployment led to mass migrations to cities.[46] The increase in the number of people in a given city looking for work put pressure on the city's infrastructure to support the larger population with no new source of income via taxes to balance the costs. Such pressure, then as now, can lead to food shortages and other basic needs going unmet.

The greater impact, however, falls on children and young adults. When the adults in a family are not able to find sufficient work, it falls to the children and young adults in the family to find work to help make ends meet. To fulfill this task, these children and young adults are expected to drop out of school to work, placing them in a precarious position.[47] Without even a basic education, the opportunities for future employment shrink dramatically, depriving these young women and men of one of the basic necessities discussed above. To follow Ellacuría's point concisely and to the present day, unemployment in the Third World is a constant because it consistently creates situations that force people to forgo the tools to escape poverty so that they can survive. Unemployment leads to generational poverty and a cycle that becomes nearly impossible to escape.

Theologically, unemployment is a sin of the world. Using language mirroring the *Agnus Dei*, the sin of the world is the sin that Jesus came to take away. Ellacuría describes the sin of the world in the following way:

> The sin of the world is the reality of this world and the people in it in negation and opposition to what God wanted of it when he created it and what he sought for it in the proclamation of the kingdom of God through the

---

46. Ellacuría, "The Kingdom of God and Unemployment," 92.
47. Ellacuría, "The Kingdom of God and Unemployment," 92.

mouth of Jesus. A reality which profoundly and universally affects the majority of people in the world and its large-scale ordering, and which is moreover the negation of God among men, can very well be described as the sin of the world.[48]

The sin of the world deals explicitly with the negation of God in reality. Exploitative economic circumstances realize the sin of the world. This fits with Ellacuría's understanding of Jesus's earthly mission, which seeks to realize the Kingdom of God and in turn, "takes away the sin of the world."[49]

In our framework of integral dehumanization and integral humanization, Ellacuría critiques the global economic system for creating situations in which unemployment is integrally dehumanizing. The current economic framework fosters unemployment as a deprivation of physical, intellectual, and social needs. Depending on the circumstances, unemployment can contribute to a deprivation of psychological needs, such as the stability that comes from a job with steady income, and spiritual needs, denying one the time and space to discern if a job is the right one to take. This is all caused by the desperation and pressure created by lacking a system of protections for those who find themselves in a situation such as unexpected and involuntary unemployment.

Ellacuría's proposed solution in this 1982 essay is an early formulation of the civilization of poverty that focuses on its relationship to unemployment:

---

48. Ellacuría, "The Kingdom of God and Unemployment," 93. While Ellacuría does not use the language of sin of the world in "Utopia and Propheticism," this concept is a common thread through his theological critique of political economy, as will be discussed below.

49. For more on Jesus's earthly mission and its importance to his salvific work, see Chapter 2 above.

Unemployment would not be debasing, if there was a new structuring of society, in which value was set not only or principally upon work called productive but also upon creative work for society. We do not need to return to the Greek world in which those who worked with their hands, or to the medieval world where contemplation and artistic work were regarded as superior to manual work or to incipient commercial work. We need to seek a new balance in which people are not subjected to economic laws but economic laws are subject to people.[50]

This emphasis on the dignity of all work emphasizes that employment is not what endows one with value; rather, it is the person doing work of any kind that endows work with value.[51] The utopian ideal expressed here shows that the civilization of poverty is meant to address the concrete problems identified by the prophetic critique. Put another way, Ellacuría's emphasis on the need for a humanizing praxis in relation to unemployment recognizes that one does not need to be dehumanized simply because one does not have a job. A society that is committed to integral human development cannot allow a person to fall through the cracks; if an economy is understood as a tool that raises the standard of living for everyone, then protections must be put in place to ensure that the economy does not leave people behind. At the risk of sounding reductive, it truly is a matter of people over profit.

The civilization of poverty, formulated through the utopian-prophetic critique of the civilization of wealth, is capable of handling concrete economic problems like that of unemploy-

---

50. Ellacuría, "The Kingdom of God and Unemployment," 96.

51. The reading of this text shows an influence of *Laborem exercens*, which was published a year earlier. While I can offer only speculation, this shows that the encyclical was a significant point of intellectual inspiration for Ellacuría. As it goes beyond the scope of this book, this line of investigation is best reserved for another research project.

ment, a problem important both to Ellacuría and the contemporary North American context. It furthers our understanding of how to see problems in light of a humanizing praxis that seeks to undo the integral dehumanization of the civilization of wealth. Moving forward, this framework must be applied to the contemporary context, articulating what this humanizing praxis looks like in the twenty-first century.

The Political Theology of Dissent

What might the civilization of poverty look like when it is realized? The underlying critique of the civilization of wealth casts doubt on the value of our current U.S. political spectrum for establishing a more just social order, of which a concrete example is the alleviation of poverty. This is shown in Ellacuría's critique of both capitalist and socialist systems in Latin American, seeing both as inadequate as they stood in his context. Emerging through Ellacuría's points, I argue for another option: a political theology of dissent, which eschews the traditional spectrum for the sake of prioritizing the praxis that addresses the concrete reality of poverty.

In Ellacuría's comparison of the East and the West as civilizations of wealth and of capital, the only difference between the two is a matter of whether that capital is controlled by private individuals or by the state.[52] Oscillating between capitalism and communism is insufficient to address the problems that are created by the exploitative nature of the civilization of wealth. Instead, "the *new political order*, prophetically sketched within the utopian horizon, is based on the attempt to overcome the political models that are the result and at the same time the support of both liberal capitalism and Marxist collectivism."[53]

---

52. Ellacuría, "Utopia and Propheticism," 40.
53. Ellacuría, "Utopia and Propheticism," 47–48 (emphasis in original).

This synthesis of the prophetic and the utopian is the foundation of a political theology of dissent. It is a dissent that rejects the conventional bilateral politico-economic spectrum because it cannot withstand the prophetic critique: neither system adequately provides a preferential option for the poor. This dissent is utopian in its rejection of the current structures because a better way can be imagined. This better way is not the centrism between two extremes but a rejection that calls for a revolution within the structure of values within the political reality one inhabits.

Revolution in this context is not a new presentation of the Marxist revolution resulting from class struggle.

> The revolution that is needed, the necessary revolution, will be the one that intends freedom deriving from and leading to justice and justice deriving and leading to freedom. This freedom must come out of liberation and not merely out of liberalization—whether economic or political liberalization—in order to overcome in this way the dominant "common evil" and build a "common good," a common good understood in contrast to the common evil and sought from a preferential option for the vast majority of people.[54]

While the revolution is anti-capitalist and anti-imperialist, it does not imply the same revolution that is called for by Marx.[55] Crucially, this revolution, while having materialist implications, does not focus on seizing the means of production. Emerging from Ellacuría's understanding of historical soteriology and the need to continue realizing the Reign of God, this revolution is focused on overcoming the common evil in whatever form it takes. The revolution is a fundamental change to reality as opposed to a redistribution of goods.

---

54. Ellacuría, "Utopia and Propheticism," 49.
55. Ellacuría, "Utopia and Propheticism," 49.

In this establishment of the common good, Ellacuría draws on Catholic Social Thought in a way that pushes the tradition forward using the demands of liberation theology that are situated in the concrete historical reality of Latin America. This revolution shifts the dynamic structures of reality in a way that is oriented for the good of the many and not only for the benefit of the few. The shift of these dynamic structures is not merely a question of who controls the factories; rather, it involves ensuring that the factories provide good for all who need them without robbing them of their inherent human dignity.

Ellacuría's understanding of the university can be a useful example of this shift. The role of the university is to provide education; and, in the Christian university, education takes shape as formation. This formation must emphasize the necessity to struggle against structural sin. On this topic, Ellacuría writes:

> This is not a matter of intentions but of verifiable deeds. If in its activity the university does not proceed by starting from our actual world as institutional sin, it is ignoring the real foundation for salvation history; if it does not struggle against structural evil, it is not in tune with the gospel.[56]

The university must work against the institutional sin that structures the world in which we live. Faculty must pursue research that combats the ideologization created by institutional sin and form their students to recognize and resist the sinful structures that they will undoubtedly encounter in their careers and lives outside the classroom. Through this kind of formation, the pos-

---

56. Ignacio Ellacuría, "Is a Different Kind of University Possible?" in John Hassett and Hugh Lacey, eds., *Towards a Society That Serves Its People: The Intellectual Contribution of El Salvador's Murdered Jesuits* (Washington, DC: Georgetown University Press, 1991), 207. For more on Ellacuría's understanding of the university, see Ignacio Ellacuría, *Escritos universitarios* (San Salvador: UCA Editores, 1999).

sibility of truly just economic relations grounded in respect for human dignity can arise. Ellacuría also rebukes the position that the opening of free markets and the liberal democracies that support them will remedy the social, political, and economic ills of a community. By emphasizing justice as the ground from which freedom grows, Ellacuría argues that freedom without justice is insufficient to remedy the common evil that is experienced by the vast majority of the Third World, which makes up 75 percent of the world's population.[57] The civilization of wealth's understanding of justice is found in the marketplace; whatever result the market can bear is found to be just because it comes from the free agreement of two autonomous parties. In deriving justice from freedom, this position ignores both the antagonism and the potential for manipulation that such an ambiguous understanding of freedom provides. Freedom must be derived from justice in order for members of the community to engage one another on a truly equal footing. When we prioritize justice in this way, the common evil can be addressed from the starting point of the common good.

The satisfaction of basic needs and the dignifying of human work are foundational for the common good's response to and healing of the common evil. The satisfaction of basic needs serves as a point of dissent from the capitalist economic model of decisions made under scarcity.[58] It refuses to accept scarcity

---

57. Ellacuría provides this statistic in "Unemployment in the Third World," 92: "If we remember that this phenomenon is massive in the Third World and that the Third World represents easily three-quarters of humanity, radical conclusions follow."

58. This position derived from the definition offered by economists Paul Samuelson and William Nordhaus: "Economics is the study of how societies use scarce resources to produce valuable goods and services and distribute them among different individuals." For more, see Paul A. Samuelson and William D. Nordhaus, *Economics*, 19th ed. (Boston: McGraw-Hill Irwin, 2010), 4–5.

as the foundational concept of reality that the ideologization of capitalism offers. While scarcity is possible, it is not the starting point for all goods, especially the basic necessities of a community. If a community operates without concern for lacking basic necessities, then the relationships within that community form in a different way. This is not to say that people would not try to take advantage of the situation; the reality of sin will always be a part of the human experience. The lack of scarcity, however, would allow the bonds of community to form under the pretense of cooperation, which raises the standard of living for the whole community. It allows for a new way to be human: one grounded in friendship and care for one another. This foundation would allow for the community to overcome an attempt to shift to a dynamic of dominance, or at the very least resist such a shift.

This leads to the point of dignified work. In dignifying human work, showing that every role in the community matters, relationships are not formed in the context of adversity or competition. Instead, bonds are grounded in cooperation, recognizing that everyone does work that has a positive impact on the community, whether it be growing food, repairing machines, educating the community, or keeping the community buildings sanitary. All work is valuable because human beings do the work. No contribution to the community is greater or less than another. This position dissents from the assumed hierarchies of wages that place greater value, and therefore greater compensation, on certain professions while leaving the less desirable positions with wages so low it is impossible to survive on them.

When both of these points of dissention are put together, we find that they reject an assumption within the logic that permeates the capitalist form of the civilization of wealth: dehumanizing poverty is a natural part of society, and, while unfortunate, it cannot be fixed. The political theology of dissent makes the prophetic call that this assumption is blatantly false. There are enough resources to ensure that people are not put in such dehumanizing positions and to allow for their human dignity to be respected. While some level of economic inequality will exist given the reality of sin, the dehumanizing poverty brought about by the civilization of wealth is not necessary. The impacts of poverty can be mitigated, thereby allowing for all persons to have their basic needs satisfied and their work humanizing.

The political theology of dissent offers a formulation of Ellacuría's utopian-prophetic critique directed at the contemporary political spectrum between the poles of capitalism and socialism. Relying on the framework of the civilization of wealth and the civilization of poverty, a political theology of dissent rejects the underlying assumption of the necessity of dehumanizing poverty. It is through this dissent that the obstructions to the Reign of God can be overcome, thereby putting us back into harmonious action with the universal Christian vocation to realize the Reign of God.

Articulating the Dissent: Three Primary Directives

In practical terms, what does the political theology of dissent look like? Grounded in prophetic word and action, the political theology of dissent is more than a system of arguments and ideas. It is a matter of attitude and praxis. The political theology of dissent consists of three primary directives: discernment of injustice, prophetic critique, and humanizing praxis. Through these three sets of practices, we can emerge with a method to remove the obstructions of the common evil and engage with the universal call to realize the Reign of God.

One may look at these directives and see an uncanny resemblance to the classic liberation theological method of "See, Judge, Act." While there is without question a genealogical connection, I am making an intentional move away from this language for a few reasons. The first reason is that "See, Judge, Act" has become more of a bumper-sticker motto than a method for theological reflection and action. While the meaning and historical significance of this method cannot be erased, they can be truncated, which is my concern. Do the terms carry the same intellectual weight today as they did decades ago? Are there not epistemological and cognitional questions that can be spurred by very simply articulated commands that call the power of their simplicity into question? To avoid all these pitfalls, I am intentionally choosing to use new terms that can perhaps more clearly, if not as simply, articulate the spirit of "See, Judge, Act."

The second, and perhaps more contentious, reason for moving beyond "See, Judge, Act" is to maintain the theological key of this methodology. "See, Judge, Act" can be ubiquitous and be applicable from secular perspectives as much as theological ones. I do not want to risk the political theology of dissent being identified as another form of secular thought that is wearing theology's clothing. By putting theological concepts such as discernment and prophetic critique at the forefront, this theological method should not be mistaken for something originating outside of the Christian, specifically Catholic, theological tradition. Instead, it should be clear that these methodological principles arise from theological reflection and Christian frameworks heavily indebted to the tradition that has formed my thought so thoroughly.

Finally, as we will see in the following expansion on the three primary directives, "See, Judge, Act" can also lead to an approach that is overly focused on short-term solutions to problems with long-term causes and effects. This is not to say that these short-term solutions do not help; they certainly do. It is important, however, for there to be a method that concurrently considers these longer-term questions so that the short-term solutions do not become a Sisyphean task. It may be helpful to consider the political theology of dissent as a complement to "See, Judge, Act"—operating toward similar goals but following different paths to deal with necessary problems. The political theology of dissent does not seek to replace "See, Judge, Act." Rather, the goal is to provide answers to a more complicated set of problems that requires a different mode of thinking and acting.[59]

Discernment of Injustice

Before one can properly dissent, one must understand precisely what one is dissenting from. This requires a process of discernment and reflection that calls for patience, understanding, and a questioning mind. It can be very easy to notice an injustice, but it requires time and effort to understand the larger picture. One's dissent must be discerned before it can be articulated or acted upon.

Take, for example, the hungry person whom one may pass on the street of Baltimore, Boston, or Milwaukee. It is very easy to see the injustice of a person lacking their daily bread. The short-term solution is also quite straightforward: feed the person! One could very easily see Pope Francis making the very same imperative. To be clear, there is nothing that says one should not feed this person. It can be as simple as buying them breakfast at a local diner, as my father would do on occasion when walking from his bus stop to work.

The problem is, however, that this person's stomach will only be full for so long before they struggle to find their next meal.

---

59. Perhaps the closest analogue to this aspect of my argument is the case M. Shawn Copeland makes in her 2004 CTSA Presidential Address, "Political Theology as Interruptive," where she offers a critique of praxis-based theologies. For more detail, see M. Shawn Copeland, "Political Theology as Interruptive," *Proceedings of the Catholic Theological Society of America* 59 (2004): 71–82.

While one can hope that the spirit of charity can be found in another person, it also behooves us to consider the structural questions involved with this person's situation. What is preventing this person from steady access to nutritious food? Why are the resources that are put in place for these situations, like a food bank, not a viable option for this person? Are the resources even available if this person were to go looking for them? These can be very complicated questions with confusing answers. This means there must be an approach that can deal with the complexity of these questions.

This is where the process of discernment comes in. Research and engaging with the questions and their political and economic answers will leave one with more data than one will know what to do with. A process of prayerful discernment, then, is the most appropriate response. Following Ellacuría's example of using the *Spiritual Exercises* to help the Jesuits of Latin America discern what the next steps for the order should be, the political theology of dissent leans on the practice of prayerful discernment to ascertain the answer to one fundamental question: where is the heart of the injustice? Amid the data, there is an answer to this question. Through prayerful reflection, we can find the element that is effectively dehumanizing great numbers of people. Once that key piece of information is found, one can begin to place the pieces of information together to have a wider understanding of the problem and its root causes.

This task is, of course, more easily said than done. Part of the discernment process may also be asking if one is even the right person to approach these problems. There may be a wide range of technical knowledge that is required to figure out some of these issues, and there may be a limit as to how much one is able to comprehend. Making the effort to understand to the ability that one can is nevertheless important. Sometimes, a fresh perspective will reveal flaws in systems that others who are more familiar with the processes miss. Also, finding the dehumanizing element, which is always a part of the heart of injustice, only requires a genuine concern for others and a determined will.

Prophetic Critique

Once one has discerned a workable understanding of the problem, the next directive is to make the prophetic critique. This critique is to be understood as prophetic in two primary ways: (1) it must be unconcerned with questions of social status and perception that do not directly impact the question of injustice at hand, and (2) it must also bring hope for the ability to rectify the injustice. This follows the example of the Hebrew Bible prophets, who critiqued the injustices in the communities of the people of Israel and offered hope of God's comfort and solace. This directive could also be understood as articulating the dissent that one has discerned.

Being unconcerned with social status and perception can be a delicate balance to find. One should seek to be respectful of social customs and respectful of other people, but one's own status should not be of concern when speaking out on the issue of injustice. This kind of critique will challenge the status quo, putting one on the outside of debates. People who are unreceptive to this constructive critique will respond negatively, with likely accusations of a lack of understanding or a clear view of the reality of the situation. One may even become the target of hate and violence. This is no different than the exclusions that the prophets faced; it must be accepted and even embraced. Ellacuría and the martyrs of El Salvador, following the way of the cross, paid the ultimate price for their prophetic critique. This is part of the universal Christian vocation: following Jesus to Golgotha, even if it may not mean our physical death.

At this point, the hopeful aspect of the prophetic must come into play, as it is hope for the end of injustice and for strength in the face of the persecution of the person making the prophetic critique. Hope in the transformative power of God's love through the realization of the Reign of God is a hope in a resurrected world that is always at hand. We human beings can always choose justice over injustice, decide to put in the work to deconstruct the structures of injustice we have built, and change for the better. This hope of conversion stems from the hope of the resurrected Christ. Sin and death no longer have power over human beings; instead, we have the freedom, should we choose to make the difficult choice to engage that freedom fully, to be in right relationship with God and our fellow human beings. Hope is the fulfillment of a promise made by love.

The Incarnation and mission of Jesus Christ are the expression of the love that promises hope. Jesus came to humanity because of love and, through love, offered hope to the poor and marginalized. Coming as a member of an oppressed group, placing himself in a context where he would know oppression and fear, was a sign of love to all those who are oppressed. The Incarnation was a promise that God had not forgotten them in their sorrows and has a special place in God's heart for them. This love promised that, though the days are cold and the nights are dark, these people forsaken by their fellow humans would be warm again. This prophetic hope must motivate the critique because we know it is possible to bring people out of the cold should we, as a larger community, be willing to do the necessary work.

Humanizing Praxis

The final directive is perhaps the easiest of the three to discuss, as it is the living out of the dissent one has discerned and articulated. Discernment, as a process, ends in action. The discernment must be lived out whether it be in following a path of vocation or committing to some other kind of decision. The action of the political theology of dissent pushes back against the common evil, removing the obstructions to the realization of the Reign of God. Since the common evil is integral dehumanization, it follows that the action that one has discerned must be a humanizing praxis. This thoughtfully considered action seeks to restore the inherent dignity of the people with whom one comes into contact by paying special attention to the ways others and/or structures may have dehumanized them.

Such action can take several shapes and may coincide with some of the actions of "See, Judge, Act." Going back to the example of my father taking a hungry, unhoused person to breakfast, we see that my father was actively acknowledging and uplifting the inherent dignity of that man on the streets of Baltimore. While my father may have been motivated more by compassion than discernment and prophetic critique, he engaged in a humanizing action nonetheless. My critique of my father is that this was not continued practice done with regularity. The political theology of dissent demands a humanizing praxis that is a continued effort over time. The praxis should be seeking to rehumanize those ravaged by the common evil, and that takes faithful commitment over time. Furthermore, how that praxis is enacted may take different forms over time as one continues to better understand the problem. While the individual actions may look different, the humanizing effect should remain a constant.

A final word on this is that much like "See, Judge, Act" the political theology of dissent is also a circular method. One should always be open to receiving new information, which in turn can lead to a new understanding of the problem. This requires more discernment, which in turn leads to a refinement of critique and shift in praxis. As long as these cycles continue, our human fallibility can be kept in check, and we will be able to operate with a level of confidence in the process of discernment. So long as this process is grounded in a Christ-like love, the Spirit will not lead us astray.

As I have developed Ellacuría's political theology in this chapter, I have focused on the utopian-prophetic critique that he developed in the concepts of the civilization of wealth and the civilization of poverty, particularly in relation to the capitalist political economy. Through this critique, a political theology of dissent, rejecting the contemporary political spectrum, critiques the assumption of the necessity of dehumanizing poverty. The critique emphasizes that dehumanizing poverty goes beyond economic inequality and becomes an expression of the common evil. The methodology behind the political theology of dissent—discernment of injustice, prophetic critique, and humanizing praxis—serves as the path that best combines the need to identify and address the structural issues undergirding the common evil as well as brings comfort to the immediate needs of those suffering. The next step, as we explore in the following chapter, applies this method to a problem facing our society and brings these steps into their most concrete form.

4

Identifying the Obstruction: Neoliberalism as the Common Evil

> Our understanding of "continuous creation" must be re-elaborated, in the knowledge that it will not be technology that saves us: endorsing utilitarian deregulation and global neoliberalism means imposing the law of the strongest as the only rule; and it is a law that dehumanizes.
>
> —Pope Francis, Message of the Holy Father to Participants in the General Assembly of the Pontifical Academy for Life
> March 3, 2025

In order to define "neoliberalism," we must untangle a conceptual knot that has been frayed and roughed up because different meanings have emerged in different contexts. In one sense, it can refer to the theories of economists such as Friedrich von Hayek and Milton Friedman.[1] Neoliberalism can also refer to the fiscal and monetary policies that were instituted by the Ronald Reagan administration in the United States and the

---

1. For examples of their economic work, see Friedrich von Hayek, *The Road to Serfdom* (Chicago: University of Chicago Press, 2007); and Milton Friedman, *Capitalism and Freedom* (Chicago: University of Chicago Press, 2020).

Margaret Thatcher government in the United Kingdom. The term has also been used as a concept in high theory by thinkers such as Michel Foucault. Another definition frames neoliberalism as the set of social and cultural values that creates the cultural matrix in which we find ourselves in the Global North in the late twentieth and early twenty-first centuries.

The working definition of neoliberalism for this chapter is: the set of cultural and social values that create a cultural matrix in which absolute economic freedom grounds the rest of culture.[2] These values center competition, the maximization of personal gain, and the understanding of the human person as primarily a firm engaging in the marketplace. These values create a culture that is framed by so-called free-market capitalism. This cultural matrix, in turn, integrally dehumanizes members of society, especially those marginalized by its economic focus.

Identifying the Injustice

As a cultural matrix, neoliberalism needs to be thoroughly engaged by theologians. Using the work of Franz Hinkelammert, Jung Mo Sung, and Keri Day, this section highlights several aspects of neoliberalism that are obstructions to the Reign of God. Together, these insights provide ample material for the necessary prophetic, theological critique.

Franz Hinkelammert and the Ideological Weapons of Death

The first critique of neoliberalism comes from the German-born, Latin American liberation theologian Franz Hinkelammert.

---

2. This definition focuses primarily on the last definition of neoliberalism discussed above while still drawing on elements from the first and second definitions. Neoliberalism as an aspect of high theory is well beyond the scope of this project as it is inactionable by praxis.

Trained in economics, Hinklehammert was an explicit critic of neoliberal policies in Latin America, notably in Chile while it was under the rule of Augusto Pinochet, who was heavily influenced by the Chicago school of economics.[3] Hinkelammert's theological critiques of neoliberalism emerged from a synthesis of economic concerns and a theology of life and death.

In Part I of *The Ideological Weapons of Death*, Hinkelammert dedicates an entire chapter to analyzing the work of Milton Friedman from a Catholic theological perspective, making three points that are significant to this project. First, he notes that Friedman is committed to the concept of freedom to the point that the freedom to murder can coexist with the freedom to live, two contradictory ideas. According to Hinkelammert, Friedman breaks from classical liberalism by rejecting the idea that certain freedoms, such as the freedom to murder, must be given up to maintain society.[4] Instead, Friedman argues that these two freedoms can coexist as long as physical force is avoided.[5] This is a distinction without a difference since murder implies some sort of physical force, whether it is an explicitly violent act or a subtler method, such as poisoning. The point, however, is clear: Friedman cannot hold that his vision of freedom is not without violence. In Hinkelammert's formulation, Friedman's conception of freedom is, at its core, "a struggle to the death, although physical force is not used."[6] All of Friedman's conceptions of value and philosophy derive from this struggle to the death, as will be shown in Hinkelammert's further critiques.

Second, Hinkelammert recognizes this struggle playing out in Friedman's understanding of human interiority as a mar-

---

3. Franz Hinkelammert, *The Ideological Weapons of Death: A Theological Critique of Capitalism* (Maryknoll, NY: Orbis Books, 1986), iv.
4. Hinkelammert, *The Ideological Weapons of Death*, 76.
5. Hinkelammert, *The Ideological Weapons of Death*, 76.
6. Hinkelammert, *The Ideological Weapons of Death*, 77.

ketplace. Hinkelammert describes Friedman's understanding of human interiority as a matter of negotiation and exchange between two subjects: the portfolio subject, who makes decisions, and a second subject, who is defined by preferences.[7] In this exchange, the portfolio subject purchases twenty-four hours from the preference subject. The portfolio subject then sells some of those hours to an outside market, namely, a public exchange market, where one is able to exchange hours of labor for a salary. With that salary, the portfolio subject is able to purchase leisure hours to return to the preference subject, who will then distribute those leisure hours in accordance with the intensity of one's preferences. From Hinkelammert's perspective, this anthropology becomes totalizing, turning human beings into mere commodities to be traded.[8]

Third, Hinkelammert critiques Friedman's understanding of charity. According to Hinkelammert, Friedman understands poverty as merely something distressing that should be alleviated, but it should only be alleviated by personal charity.[9] Hinkelammert argues that Friedman frames charity as something that can be done by anyone to the same effect, so a self-interested individual need not feel obligated to do the charitable giving herself.[10] Hinkelammert rejects this conception of charity outright, instead showing a preference for the charity of St. Vincent de Paul.[11] The Vincentian conception of charity, which recognizes the importance of the human person in poverty, seeks

---

7. Hinkelammert, *The Ideological Weapons of Death*, 78. One could understand the preference subject as a form of the appetitive part of the soul from the allegory of the chariot in Plato's *Phaedrus*, §§246a-254e.

8. Hinkelammert, *The Ideological Weapons of Death*, 80. Hinkelammert's analysis continues but begins to enter into the intricacies of Marxist analysis, which is beyond the scope of the argument here.

9. Hinkelammert, *The Ideological Weapons of Death*, 95.

10. Hinkelammert, *The Ideological Weapons of Death*, 95.

11. Hinkelammert, *The Ideological Weapons of Death*, 95.

both to bring the person out of dehumanizing material poverty and to enter into community with the poor person, thereby affirming one's own humanity.[12] By contrast, Friedman's understanding of charity never recognizes the human face of poverty, nor does it recognize how the absolute self-interested freedom in his system perpetuates and worsens this problem.

Simply put, for Hinkelammert, a theology of life—namely, a theology of liberation—grounds an adequate theological response to the life and death struggle of neoliberal capitalism.[13] Hinkelammert builds his theology of life and death upon Gospel stories of Christ's death and resurrection as well as on Pauline writings about embodiment, which understand salvation from death as the heart of the theological project in the midst of questions of empire, consumerism, and the slavery of sin.[14]

Jung Mo Sung and *Desire, Market, Religion*

Jung Mo Sung develops Hinkelammert's themes from a theology of life within contemporary circumstances.[15] Practically, Sung's work reflects a precrisis neoliberal order, which is helpful for two reasons. First, he reflects on neoliberalism at a point of its

---

12. Hinkelammert, *The Ideological Weapons of Death*, 96.
13. Hinkelammert, *The Ideological Weapons of Death*, 226–28. Hinkelammert's theological reflections on topics of crucifixion, Eucharist, poverty, and Catholic social teaching and their relation to capitalism are very interesting and provide a great deal of material to reflect upon how to understand the tensions behind holding one's position as both a Catholic and a Marxist. An analysis of the merits of Hinkelammert's commitments as a Catholic and Marxist thinker, while very stimulating, distract from my purposes here, and therefore must be left for another project.
14. Hinkelammert, *The Ideological Weapons of Death*, 127–52.
15. It is important to note that the English edition of *Desire, Market, and Religion*, the version of the text that will be cited throughout this discussion, is composed of the original Brazilian text published in 1998, along with two additional chapters written in 2003 and 2006. Jung Mo Sung, *Desire, Market, Religion* (London: SCM Press, 2007), 4.

established dominance, showing a development in theological critique without a focus on the structural crisis to come. Second, Sung, following Hinkelammert, shows how figures within Latin American liberation theology were acutely aware of neoliberalism's dangers even before theologians in the Global North were awakened to the problems by the crisis of 2007–2008. As we have already engaged one of these Latin American liberation theologians—Ignacio Ellacuría—in this book, Sung's analysis heightens our attention on the importance of theology interfering with economics and the market. The former has become the theology of the neoliberal order, and the latter is its idol.

For Sung, theology must interfere with economics. He starts with Thomas Aquinas's assertion that human beings cannot know God in Godself and claims that theological reflections must, then, explore different images of God to help further our understanding of God as much as possible within the bounds of finitude.[16] Sung pursues an image of God as creator and giver of life, citing creation accounts in Genesis as well as Jesus's sayings in the Gospel of John.[17] From the Gospel of Matthew, he identifies material necessities of life, specifically food, drink, clothing, safe housing, freedom, "and affection or acceptance."[18] Each of us are, then, judged by God on the basis of how one provides these needs for those on the margins of society, who can never repay or reciprocate these actions. Since the way these material necessities are produced, distributed, and consumed is within the realm of economics, it follows that theology must interfere with economic forces that perpetuate forces of death.[19]

Sung calls on Christian theologians to recognize the implicit theological claims that are made by neoliberal thinkers and

---

16. Sung, *Desire, Market, and Religion*, 8–9.
17. Sung, *Desire, Market, and Religion*, 9.
18. Sung, *Desire, Market, and Religion*, 9–10.
19. Sung, *Desire, Market, and Religion*, 10.

that shape a theology of neoliberalism. This theology is not a Christian one, strictly speaking. Rather, it is a theology of the market that has troubling similarities to Christian theological concerns, particularly dealing with questions of death, fallenness, and sacrifice.

The first neoliberal theological tenet is a promise to eliminate death via technological progress. According to Sung, neoliberalism is built around the mythical idea that the technological and economic engine of progress is in a perpetually forward motion; progress cannot be stopped and is always moving us closer to paradise.[20] Problematically, this vision of progress eliminates the need for limits on human actions.[21] Without a need for limits, progress then supposedly creates a utopia that ends violent death.[22] The understanding of death itself is transformed in neoliberal society. Instead of seeing death as a natural part of life that can only be rectified in terms of salvation through Christ,[23] individuals formed by neoliberal culture see death as a failure of medical science that can be avoided if enough time is given for progress to cure a particular malady.[24] From a neoliberal perspective, death is a sign of losing the competition of life, and this loss must be put off. The Christian, seeing the powerful message of the crucifixion, knows that death is unavoidable but not the end.

---

20. Sung, *Desire, Market, and Religion*, 12.
21. Sung, *Desire, Market, and Religion*, 13.
22. Sung, *Desire, Market, and Religion*, 13.
23. Sung appears to be alluding to 1 Corinthians 15 and Paul's discussion of salvation as victory over death through Christ's sacrificial death for humanity's sins. This line of thinking continues throughout the Christian tradition, taking a new form in Latin American liberation theology, given the grim reality of death seen by these thinkers. During a lecture at Marquette University on April 20, 2015, Gustavo Gutiérrez spoke of the significance of "people dying before their time," showing how this question is in the background of his and other liberation theologians' thought.
24. Sung, *Desire, Market, and Religion*, 13.

The second neoliberal theological tenet is the question of original sin, particularly as it is presented by Friedrich von Hayek. His understanding of an "original sin" comes from a similar pattern of logic as the traditional Christian theological understanding of original sin as a rejection of God's love that leads to a broken relationship between God and humanity. Sung describes von Hayek's understanding of what could be considered an original sin in economics as the presumption of knowing more about the market and its workings than is possible and breaking the laws of the market based on these presumptions.[25] As Sung puts it, the problem for von Hayek is that attempts to intervene in a situation only make the situation worse. The "temptation to do good" is the fundamental starting point for economic sin.[26] This neoliberal approach reduces the natural law precept of "do good and avoid evil" to a simple avoidance of evil, removing an impetus for active pursuit of good.[27] Prioritizing avoidance of evil without an injunction to also do good is coherent with the significance of "freedom" in neoliberal thought, and it mirrors attitudes toward regulation of the marketplace. The principle of the avoidance of evil alone provides an imperative to self-interested non-interference that allows for the injustices that one may encounter to continue under the assumption that the market will settle matters itself.

The third and final theological tenet of neoliberalism that is relevant for the current discussion regards necessary sacrifices. Sung challenges neoliberal theology to account for the violence that is done to innocents for the sake of progress.[28] From the neoliberal perspective, these are necessary sacrifices

---

25. Sung, *Desire, Market, and Religion*, 15.
26. Sung, *Desire, Market, and Religion*, 15.
27. Sung, *Desire, Market, and Religion*, 16.
28. Sung, *Desire, Market, and Religion*, 18.

that make it possible for the market to function.²⁹ These "necessary" sacrifices are contrary to a Christian notion of sacrifice, which involves a voluntary act of self-giving for the sake of another in an interpersonal relationship.³⁰ Neoliberal theology's notion of sacrifice hinges on involuntary victims and those who are willing to sacrifice said victims for the sake of a profitable transaction. The neoliberal "necessary sacrifices" seem to be more in line with Robert Daly's understanding of sacrifice in the ancient world: the destruction of the sacrifice is merely a fact of the ceremony, not something to be celebrated or even acknowledged. This is similar to the way the "necessary sacrifices" to the market are considered.³¹

These theological tenets of neoliberalism shape and are shaped by the context of a globalized economy that consistently victimizes the poor, particularly in the Global South. The relationships between the neoliberal theological vision and Christian theology broadly understood may be difficult to discern. For Sung, building on the work of Hinkelammert and Hugo Assmann, Christian theology must recognize in neoliberal theology "the idolatry of the market."³² Assmann's critiques of the idolatry of the market range from Marxist and socialist thought to focusing on material practices like the fetishism of idols.³³ Sung develops Assmann's multifaceted critiques, showing how neoliberalism's "necessary sacrifices" are made to a

---

29. Sung, *Desire, Market, and Religion*, 18.
30. This brief description of the Christian notion of sacrifice does not represent the wealth of scholarship on the topic, which would distract from the primary argument of this dissertation. For further reading on Christian conceptions of sacrifice, see Robert J. Daly, S.J., *Sacrifice Unveiled: The True Meaning of Christian Sacrifice* (New York: T&T Clark, 2009).
31. Daly, *Sacrificed Unveiled*, 27.
32. Sung, *Desire, Market, and Religion*, 110. For Assmann's full argument, see Hugo Assmann, *Teología desde la práxis de la liberació: ensayo teológico desde la América dependiente* (Salamanca: Ed. Sígueme, 1973).
33. Sung, *Desire, Market, and Religion*, 110–11.

deity of market processes, whose favor is granted to those who avoid falling into "the temptation to do good."[34]

With Sung, Christian theologians can begin to recognize how neoliberal culture takes on and modifies religious ideas. The idolatry of the market and the other theological tenets of neoliberalism are aspects of a neoliberal systematic theology that poses problems for Christian theology. By showing the theological claims at work in the thought of von Hayek and others, Sung calls Christian theologians to recognize that theological ethics or moral theology are not the only ways to engage economic ideas and political decision-making. Theologians' work must expand beyond questions of ethics without losing the concrete details that impact the lives of those who are being sacrificed upon the market's altar.

Hinkelammert and Sung trace neoliberal ideology from its infancy in the mid-1970s to its maturity in the late 1990s and early 2000s. Keri Day moves theology through the failure of several banks that were "too big to fail" in the late 2000s. Their failure sent the entire economy, connected by these financial institutions and their networks, into a freefall that required government intervention through a practice called "quantitative easing."[35] Writing through and in the aftermath of the economic crisis, Day traces a paradigm shift that demonstrated neoliberalism's failures and its widespread consequences.

Keri Day and *Religious Resistance to Neoliberalism*

In *Religious Resistance to Neoliberalism: Womanist and Black Feminist Perspectives*, Keri Day articulates several anthropo-

---

34. Sung, *Desire, Market, and Religion*, 111–12.
35. In quantitative easing, a nation's central bank, the Federal Reserve of the United States in this case, purchases government securities, increasing the money supply to encourage lending. While most businesses would recover in the decade following the 2007–2008 crisis, the widespread impacts of the crisis and related policy decisions are still being felt by the rest of the population.

logical concerns about how neoliberalism forms a person's self-understanding and interpersonal relationships.[36] Her discussion of the acquiring mode, the loss of *eros* in neoliberal society, and hope and love as revolutionary social praxis are instructive for our recognition of neoliberalism as the common evil.

For Day, individual change and social change are not distinct phenomena.[37] She investigates what she calls the acquiring mode, describing it as "a neoliberal way of being that defines human meaning based on the material things one can acquire. This mode then shapes the consciousness of the human subject within diverse market societies."[38] Day unpacks this definition by noting how neoliberal capitalism often commodifies the human being through unmitigated competitive impulses, causing one to understand nonmarket concepts, such as trust and love, in terms of market practices, which imply material objects and objectification.[39] The problem with relating to everything as a material object is that material objects cannot give, share, love, or create, which are all actions requiring an acting subject, namely, other humans.[40] These actions, which are intended to be done in relation to other acting subjects, are what Day means when she says that "to be human is to 'alive.'"[41] This understanding of "alive" is to be engaged in either productive activity

---

36. It is important to note here that Day understands neoliberal as a term that goes beyond Western capitalism in contemporary times, with variations in Chinese state capitalism and the monetarist approaches in Latin America. While Day makes these distinctions, it does not impact my argument given that her analysis applies to all variations of neoliberalism. For more on Day's distinctions in the introduction, see Keri Day, *Religious Resistance to Neoliberalism: Womanist and Black Feminist Perspectives* (London: Palgrave Macmillan, 2015), 1–17.
37. Day, *Religious Resistance to Neoliberalism*, 47.
38. Day, *Religious Resistance to Neoliberalism*, 47.
39. Day, *Religious Resistance to Neoliberalism*, 48–50.
40. Day, *Religious Resistance to Neoliberalism*, 50.
41. Day, *Religious Resistance to Neoliberalism*, 50.

or nonalienated activity, in which one experiences herself as a subject and is able to understand herself, her productivity, and the result of that productivity as one.[42] Alive stands in opposition to alienated activity, where one is not able to experience herself as a subject of her activity.[43]

To illustrate Day's point, let us take an example of a carpenter building a table to give as a gift for her friend's family who just moved into a new home. This act is productive, in that the carpenter is practicing her craft. The carpenter can experience this as a nonalienated activity, where she recognizes her skill at work, sees the creation of bringing an object to life from pieces of wood by her own hand, and knows that there is continuity between herself, her actions, and the table she is constructing that will be used by a family to share meals and have conversations. In other words, the carpenter is doing more than building a table; she is sharing her gifts with those she loves to help facilitate more giving, sharing, and loving in a way that is fundamental to human relationships: table fellowship. She can also experience her work as alienating activity, where she builds a table to sell as a part of a large retailer's mass-produced collection, never seeing herself as the subject of her actions but merely as a machine that is tasked to produce another product for sale on the market so she can pay her debts and buy a new television. From Day's insight, we can recognize how the acquiring mode replaces the nonalienating and life-giving activity with alienating activity, which destroys what it means to be human.[44] Destruction of humanity on the individual level eventually leads to a society that is characterized by individuals who "presume that the acquiring of wealth says something about who is

---

42. Day, *Religious Resistance to Neoliberalism*, 50–51.
43. Day, *Religious Resistance to Neoliberalism*, 51.
44. Day, *Religious Resistance to Neoliberalism*, 51.

worthy or commendable and who is not praiseworthy within society."[45] In short, neoliberal culture transforms human value into something that can be measured on a sheet of assets and liabilities.

The second aspect of Day's analysis that is relevant for this project is her analysis of the loss of *eros* in neoliberal culture. *Eros* is not merely a pornographic sexual desire but a wholistic, passionate, unifying love that desires the beloved.[46] Citing Karen Baker-Fletcher, Day understands *eros* as a love that recognizes humanity's embodied, creaturely status and has the ability to heal both the body and the soul.[47] Depriving human beings of their ability to live, neoliberalism emphasizes a "sensation without feeling," which contributes to the reduction of the complexity of *eros* to mere sexual desire that can be fulfilled without interpersonal connection.[48] Day illustrates this point in a powerful way, writing:

> The erotic is a passionate life force and creative energy that fuels all of our endeavors and loving acts of labor in the world. The horror of neoliberal societies is that it defines the good and beautiful in terms of profit rather than in terms of human connection and care, which robs us of erotic value and power within our ways of being and living. We are emotionally numb to ourselves and others, unable to feel anything because our false "good" is bound up with the reckless pursuit of money and its concomitant alienating ways of acting (social distrust, lack of care, etc.). The numbness of feeling that neoliberal society produces cuts us off from the emotional, connective power needed

---

45. Day, *Religious Resistance to Neoliberalism*, 53.
46. Day, *Religious Resistance to Neoliberalism*, 81.
47. Day, *Religious Resistance to Neoliberalism*, 81.
48. Day, *Religious Resistance to Neoliberalism*, 82.

to transform our societies into just and compassionate communities.[49]

Through the acquisitive mode and alienation, neoliberalism deprives humans of the erotic that allows us to connect to one another. Denying our connection further deprives us of having a society that is built upon compassion and justice and replaces those foundational pillars with empty acquisition and competition. Finally, Day calls her readers to hope and love as concrete practices of resistance to neoliberalism.[50] In understanding hope and love as more than just abstract concepts that are confined to homilies or sympathy cards, Day provides a groundwork on how to make resistance to neoliberalism more than just a political act. Hope and love are necessary praxis as one seeks to emulate Christ, forming resistance to neoliberalism as a religiously liberating act.

Together, Hinkelammert, Sung, and Day provide us with helpful diagnoses of the problems of neoliberalism as a cultural matrix. From Hinkelammert, we draw an analysis of the complications of Friedman's conception of freedom, his truncation of the human person that reduces them to a stock portfolio, and his critique of charity. Sung's diagnosis provides an understanding of the neoliberal vision of escaping death, original sin, and "necessary" sacrifices of the poor and the marginalized. Day's constructive critique emphasizes the way that human connection is fundamentally broken and human desire is corrupted

---

49. Day, *Religious Resistance to Neoliberalism*, 82.
50. While Day dedicates two chapters of the monograph to love and hope, her articulation of how these two theological virtues function as social practices is not as important to the present argument at this point in the project as the fact that she names them as practices. For more on Day's articulation of love and hope as social practices, see Day, *Religious Resistance to Neoliberalism*, 105–59.

by neoliberalism, which requires a response of love and hope as concrete practices. A prophetic critique of the neoliberal cultural matrix emerges from these rich theological diagnoses that show neoliberalism to be a major factor in and cause of integral dehumanization on multiple levels. In short, with the injustice identified, we can construct a meaningful critique to empower humanizing praxis.

Prophetic Critique

St. John Paul II, in his apostolic exhortation *Ecclesia in America*, offers a concise, insightful understanding of the problem of neoliberalism in terms of dehumanization. He writes:

> More and more, in many countries of America, a system known as "neoliberalism" prevails; based on a purely economic conception of man, this system considers profit and the law of the market as its only parameters, to the detriment of the dignity of and the respect due to individuals and peoples. At times this system has become the ideological justification for certain attitudes and behavior in the social and political spheres leading to the neglect of the weaker members of society. Indeed, the poor are becoming ever more numerous, victims of specific policies and structures which are often unjust.[51]

The former pontiff highlighted the fundamental problem of neoliberalism: it truncates the human person to only one materialistic aspect and expects people to act accordingly. If one cannot meet those materialist standards, then one is to be left by the wayside. This is fundamentally unjust. In highlighting the American church, John Paul II recognized the influence that the remaining international superpower in the wake of the Cold

---

51. St. John Paul II, *Ecclesia in America* (Vatican City: Libreria Editrice Vaticana, 1999), §56.

War could have upon the world. He was concerned that the influence of American religion would eventually take hold in other places around the world as America's influence expands.

He was right. The neoliberal ideology that has become part and parcel of the United States' economic policies have gone on to affect the rest of the world.

Importantly, this critique is not made from another politico-economic ideological perspective. The motivating factors of this critique are grounded in the tradition of Catholic Social Thought: integral human development and the preferential option for the poor. By using these two concepts as the foundational planks of the prophetic critique, we can avoid the appearance of simply attempting to push another ideological vision of political economy. Instead, this critique comes from a love for the gospel and a desire to help bring about the Reign of God.

Neoliberalism as First Philosophy

The phrase "first philosophy" refers to an investigation into those things that are most fundamental. Throughout the history of philosophy, there have been various approaches to this question. For Aristotle, metaphysics served as first philosophy as he sought to answer the "what is it?" question. Descartes understood epistemology as first philosophy, seeking to understand the certainty of knowledge before considering other issues. Emmanuel Lévinas argued for ethics as first philosophy, emphasizing that our responsibility to the other takes our primary focus.

I argue that neoliberalism is our culture's first philosophy. We, as a cultural whole, assume neoliberal propositions as fundamental to the choices we make. The primary assumptions that we make include an acceptance and celebration of extreme selfishness as a primary anthropological trait, neoliberal economic logic as a framework for decision-making, and a glorification of profit as the highest good.

The first principle, the acceptance and celebration of extreme selfishness as a primary anthropological trait, is easily seen throughout our culture. While we express a moral indignation at someone who acts selfishly, we accept it as a natural state. Acts of altruism are seen as out of the norm and worthy of note. Humanitarian projects, for example, are unexpected, while the greed associated with the hoarding of wealth is simply assumed. The altruism of the Bill and Melinda Gates Foundation is seen to be remarkable and worthy of celebration, while the wealth that built that foundation is assumed as natural. The idea that a president would charge the Secret Service, and thus the taxpayer, for staying at his own hotel while on the job protecting him is appalling, but it is not unexpected. On a smaller scale, we expect someone to see others as agents looking out only for themselves, each of us seeking to maximize our own gain.

The 2001 Oscar-winning film *A Beautiful Mind*, a biopic of John Nash, the 1994 Nobel Laureate in Economics, depicts Nash's major economic theory rather simply. In the film, Nash's theory contends that the pursuit of one's selfish desires, so long as it does not impede the selfish desires of others in a group context, can lead to the highest good of everyone involved. While this does not adequately account for the nuance of the real Nash's economic theory, it is telling that the filmmaker frames the theory in a way that he sees that the general public could understand: in terms of selfishness. If our popular culture is couching an anthropology in terms of selfishness, then we at least tacitly accept that human beings are inherently selfish *and* that this is acceptable.

The second principle of neoliberalism as first philosophy is that neoliberal economic logic is the foundation for decision-making. This principle is derived from several sources, beginning with the idea that economic freedom is the condition of the possibility of all freedom. While Friedrich von Hayek expresses the theoretical foundations of this idea in *The Road to Serfdom*, cultural embodiment totalizes it into a full-blown anthropology. We understand ourselves as economic units, and our language explicitly shows this to be the case. We "invest" in ourselves, emphasize "time is money," and think of how we "budget" our time. This language seems innocuous, but it betrays the way in which we think about our world in capitalist terms and underscores the idea that the framework of economic freedom is how we understand the rest of our freedom. If we see ourselves primarily as business firms, as Friedman argued above, and allocate our physical, mental, and emotional capacities as if they were budgetary resources, then we fundamentally lose something in our understanding of the human being as an integral creature.

A third and final principle of neoliberalism as first philosophy addresses profit as the highest good. While we explicitly claim that happiness is the highest good in life, our cultural understanding of happiness and success is grounded in the fulfillment of the acquisitive desire for material goods. Those goods are almost always a result of profit, which is technically defined as the positive difference between one's revenue and liabilities/debts. In our society, the hallmark of success is culturally gauged by the financial gains that one has made in terms of our property, such as owning one's home and having a nice car. While there are particular goods that come with owning such property outright, such as the security of not being able to be evicted from one's home, these are not the only markers that one is flourishing. A person can be thriving spiritually and mentally while still making payments on a car and renting an apartment. By discounting these elements, we again miss a fundamental anthropological point: truncating the human person to only their material aspects.

When these three elements come together, they present a set of social and cultural values that open the door to integral dehumanization on a broad scale. This first philosophy of neoliberalism views both the human person and the society in which they live through lenses of competition and selfishness, merely dressed up in niceties and paying lip service to humanizing ideals.

The neoliberal values of contemporary society are harmful. We have internalized them as members of this society, which leads to dehumanizing attitudes, thoughts, and actions. From these points, we must conclude that neoliberalism has the potential to be a manifestation of the common evil.

Neoliberalism as Integral Dehumanization

At this point, we must test our hypothesis. Integral dehumanization depends on the deprivation of the integral needs that are required for human flourishing. In the following section, I examine how neoliberalism contributes to each of the five kinds of dehumanization that denote the common evil.

First, physical needs must be examined. Neoliberal cultural assertions, especially in the U.S. context, emphasize self-reliance and the expectation that one is to be able to provide for oneself in all aspects, especially financially. When we consider a situation like that of Amy discussed in chapter 3, we notice that it can be very easy for one financial emergency to knock over the already precariously balanced house of cards. A common result of this fall is a situation of temporary or prolonged homelessness.

When taking a critical look at the issue of homelessness, the physical danger becomes very pronounced. According to the U.S. Department of Housing and Urban Development, 653,104 people experienced homelessness in 2023, with 39.3 percent of that number being unsheltered.[52] Over half a million people

---

52. The U.S. Department of Housing and Urban Development, *The 2023 Annual Homelessness Assessment Report to Congress* (Washington, DC, 2023), 10, https://www.huduser.gov/portal/sites/default/files/pdf/2023-AHAR-Part-1.pdf.

were without a fixed place to sleep, and over a quarter of a million had no shelter whatsoever. This number is, quite frankly, astounding. These people also faced mortal danger, and, as a society, we show very little care for them. This offers one of several possible examples that show how neoliberal culture, with its economic anthropology, dehumanizes those without the financial resources to fit the cultural standards.

Second, we must consider the psychological dehumanization that is caused by neoliberalism. From the criteria for dehumanization in the first chapter, we must recognize how neoliberalism shapes how one views oneself. How does neoliberalism cause us to see ourselves as less than human? One way in which this occurs is how neoliberal culture impacts our ability to relate to one another in light of the foundational concept of competition. Philosopher Michelle Maiese, whose work looks at the impact of neoliberalism on mental-health education, emphasizes the significance of the neoliberal ideals of "mutually antagonistic individualism and competition."[53] These ideals erode our ability to seek out help from others, causing mental-health issues to develop further. When one cannot help but see oneself as in constant competition with everyone else, one will be less inclined to talk to a friend about one's problems, let alone a professional clinician. In addition to these attitudes regarding help-seeking, Maiese notes that the impact on children is particularly difficult. The anxiety and emotional instability of children who grow up in the neoliberal context come to a head when the child finds themselves in high-pressure situations, such as trying to build an academic resume that is worthy of admission to a top university.[54]

Maiese's framework highlights yet another angle of a recurring theme: neoliberal anthropology is a truncated view of

---

53. Michelle Maiese, "Neoliberalism and Mental Health Education," *Journal of Philosophy of Education* 56 (2022): 67–77.

54. Maiese, "Neoliberalism and Mental Health Education," 70–71.

the human person. This truncated view of the human person is clearly causing psychological distress in the children whom Maiese discussed in her article. The damage multiplies as this view becomes internalized. Concretely, understanding oneself solely as a competitor who lives in antagonistic relationships with other competitors fundamentally changes the ways that one can relate to others and to oneself. More fundamental anthropological claims, such as the human person as a social creature in need of community, contradict the antagonist competition. Neoliberal self-interpretation does not allow for genuine community to develop and causes further dehumanization by depriving the human person of the fundamental need for connection. Neoliberalism's psychological dehumanization is intimately related to its social dehumanization.

A third element, social dehumanization, may seem blatantly obvious from the earlier discussion of Hinkelammert, Sung, and Day. In particular, neoliberalism's social dehumanization is focused on the poor. Those without the means to engage fully with the market are seen as lesser persons, or they may very well be ignored in their entirety. The reality of systemic suffering on a large scale is ignored for one reason or another, and individuals, which is where the neoliberal wants to place all of the focus, are blamed for their own circumstances. While there could be a form of scapegoating that is occurring in this blame, it is not the primary issue at play in this iteration of social dehumanization. Instead, neoliberalism emphatically exercises a group bias that celebrates the wealthy and their continued accumulation of wealth and power.

Part of the challenge of engaging with neoliberalism on this point is, as theologian Vincent Miller eloquently explains, that neoliberalism does not see classes, only individuals.[55] As hinted

---

55. Vincent J. Miller, "Neoliberalism and Theological Anthropology: The Hidden Formation of Student Loans and Dating Apps," in *The T&T Clark*

at above, the neoliberal is only able to conceive of the individual and refuses to fully recognize social relationships outside of the market relationships that are necessarily contracted to accomplish individual projects. The only understanding of the collective is the firm, which is just a market actor on a larger scale.[56] Firms act as individuals and, if the U.S. Supreme Court decision in *Citizens United v. Federal Election Commission* is to be believed, are as capable of political free speech as any human U.S. citizen. Even in the context of the organization, the firm is still treated as a single actor in the market, not as a group of people in a society. It is fitting to quote one of neoliberalism's great proponents, Margaret Thatcher, here: "There is no such thing as society."[57]

At this point, it is fair to ask, "If neoliberalism places such a focus on individuals, then how can it be *socially* dehumanizing?" Neoliberalism seemingly cannot abide the handing down of social relationships through the generations. Miller's critique is worth quoting at length:

> All of this presumes that each generation begins with a clean slate in its market position. If they have the proper skills and motivations, they have an equal chance at success in the marketplace. Thus, historic injustices are liquidated into a frame that sees only contemporary opportunities that anyone can choose to pursue or ignore and do so well or poorly. But even by the narrowest economic measures, minoritized communities have a profound, intergenerational legacy of fewer assets.[58]

Handbook of Theological Anthropology, ed. Mary Ann Hinsdale, I.H.M., and Stephen Okey (London: T&T Clark, 2021), 391–93.

56. Miller, "Neoliberalism and Theological Anthropology," 392.

57. "Interview for *Women's Own* ('no such thing as society')," Margaret Thatcher Foundation, https://www.margaretthatcher.org/document/106689.

58. Miller, "Neoliberalism and Theological Anthropology," 392.

This point from Miller is the key to understanding neoliberalism as socially dehumanizing. Social dehumanization begins when a group of people, singled out as individuals but singled out for the same reasons, are blamed for situations of economic struggle over which they have no control. When the historical conditions that shape reality are ignored, people who live in compromised positions are blamed for things that were never their fault to begin with. By actively severing generations from one another and hyperfixating on the present to the point of isolation, neoliberal culture is fundamentally socially dehumanizing.

Fourth, neoliberalism's intellectual dehumanization ingrains this isolation. From a truncated anthropology, neoliberalism truncates human knowledge solely to that which is profitable and quantifiable. There are several ways in which this occurs, but we will focus on two: the shift to standardized testing in K–12 (kindergarten through twelfth grade) education in the United States and the ideologization of higher education as a merely financial transaction.

In the last twenty-five years of K–12 education in the United States, a major shift toward standardized testing as the primary emphasis in education has occurred. Concretely, a system was put into place under the No Child Left Behind Act of 2001 that linked public school funding to test scores.[59] This led to an emphasis on forming good test takers rather than developing the intellectual curiosity of children that would continue to flourish as they grew. This shift has reshaped education in dehumanizing ways as students are not adequately taught, for example, how to develop the reading attention span to engage with long-form literature, both fiction and nonfiction.[60] This

---

59. For details, see No Child Left Behind Act of 2001, H.R. 1, 107th Cong. (2001), https://www.congress.gov/bill/107th-congress/house-bill/1.

60. This has particularly come to light in college classrooms, even those

failure to develop this foundational skill dehumanizes students as it makes it extremely difficult for them to fulfill a significant part of their intellectual development and flourishing. It also fails these students in preparing them for higher education, informed social participation, and healthy curiosity. Together with myriad other primary educational failures, neoliberalism's truncated pedagogy has even led to a deformed vision of what a college education should be.

Gerald Beyer describes this worldview's effects on higher education in the following way: "Though not true of all students, many view higher education as simply another good to be purchased in the marketplace. Faculty members are often seen as 'cashiers' who should above all strive for the 'customer satisfaction' of their high-paying customers, i.e., students and their parents."[61] Beyer draws our attention to how another formative part of a person's experience in early adulthood and the great intellectual development that occurs during that time have been commoditized and turned into something less than humanizing. Neoliberalism values intellectual malformation, and the educational structures are consequentially damaged by these values. This truncated outlook on education that characterizes neoliberal culture once again shows that neoliberalism is intellectually dehumanizing.

Finally, we must address neoliberalism's fundamental spiritual dehumanization. This comes in two main forms: the implicit theology of neoliberalism and the failure of the universal church to reject the ideologization of neoliberalism. Both

---

institutions such as Georgetown University and Columbia University. For details on this, see Rose Horowitch, "The Elite College Students Who Can't Read Books," *Atlantic Monthly*, November 2024, 14–16.

61. Gerald J. Beyer, *Just Universities: Catholic Social Teaching Confronts Corporatized Higher Education* (New York: Fordham University Press, 2021), 15.

of these aspects create a form of spiritual dehumanization that most clearly articulates how neoliberalism is an obstruction to the Reign of God.

The implied theology of neoliberalism sacrifices the poor and the vulnerable for the greater profit of all, offers salvation from death through technological progress, redefines original sin in terms of improper economic attitudes and actions, and glorifies the acquisitive desire over and above the unity-seeking *eros*. These are, quite simply, idols that detract from the loving God who desires to be in relationship with us. Neoliberalism offers an idolatrous ideologization that spits in the face of the Christian ethos and obligation to the poor and marginalized by ignoring the importance of our relationality with God, creation, and one another. It undermines the relational Augustinian framework of Christian theology that guides us toward the richness of faith seeking understanding by insisting on a dehumanizing and toxic ideology of individual isolation as success.

Tragically, the universal church has abjectly failed to reject neoliberalism and its ideologized framework. Rather than guiding their flocks to more humanizing and justice-oriented ways of understanding the economy, competition, relationality, and hope, church leaders have irresponsibly allowed neoliberal ideologization to proliferate. Though certainly not alone among Christian traditions, the Catholic Church has attempted to embrace, justify, and even baptize aspects of neoliberalism within itself. When leaders, from Roman Curia to pulpit, have not felt comfortable with explicitly embracing idolatry, they have let impotent lip-service to the gospel serve as a cover for utter silence on the concrete issues of suffering and death that are hailed as "necessary" for the well-being of the market and the advance of neoliberal values.

Church history is riddled with stories of those who are willing to bend the gospel message to benefit the wealthy and powerful of their day. If history teaches us anything, it would be that this kind of theological mental gymnastics is to be expected as new paradigms emerge. Today, neoliberalism's allies in the church offer subtle, selective readings of the Catholic Church's magisterial teachings as a way of elevating neoliberal ideologization of capital and wealth above ideologies that read Scripture and tradition with an open heart to the poor and marginalized, and critique earthly power and its oppressive practices. With subtle and specialized theological interpretation, the church has also entered into open and explicit partnership with neoliberal political forces, such as the alliance between the Religious Right and the Republican Party that has led to the "Christian" argument for the support of Donald Trump. This alliance is a case study of neoliberalism's appeal to false salvific figures, indicting neoliberal Catholicism for both its idolatry and its willing partnership with its former Evangelical persecutors for the sake of further social persecution of other marginalized peoples.[62] Once again, this is an affront to the gospel and looks nothing like the message preached by Jesus of Nazareth and his apostles.

On the other hand, the silence of some church authorities is also familiar in the struggle for justice. Dr. Martin Luther King Jr. remarked on the silence of clergymen in the struggle for civil rights. He wrote:

> When I was suddenly catapulted into the leadership of the bus protest in Montgomery, Alabama, a few years ago, I felt we would be supported by the white church. I felt that the white ministers, priests and rabbis of the South would

---

62. For more on neoliberalism's false soteriology, see Andrew T. Vink, "El neoliberalismo como una falsa soteriologia," in *La teología ante los nuevos movimientos sociales*, ed. Sebastian Pittl, Jean Nicklas Collet, Thomas Fornet-Ponse, and José Sols Lucia (Bogota: Sal Terrae Editores, 2023), 152–68.

be among our strongest allies. Instead, some have been outright opponents, refusing to understand the freedom movement and misrepresenting its leaders; all too many others have been more cautious than courageous and have remained silent behind the anesthetizing security of stained glass windows.[63]

The anesthetizing security of stained glass windows demands reflection on the struggle against neoliberalism. The calm silence of the sanctuary can be a place of peace and renewal, but it must also force us to leave its doors with a mission of service to those who have been rejected by society. When the beautifully colored light that streams through the windows numbs us to the pain and suffering that our cultural matrix inflicts upon us all, especially the poor, the house of worship can only support a negative peace at best. As King has noted, negative peace favors the absence of tension, while positive peace is rooted in active justice. Silence in the face of neoliberal idolatry and dehumanization may feel comforting as an absence of tension from or active participation in the suffering of others. Yet this comfort dehumanizes the poor by valuing a bourgeois Christianity that fails to inspire, let alone pursue prophetic action.

Both of these paths, embrace and silence, lead to the same place: the spiritual dehumanization of congregations and the reduction of the poor to characters in an empty platitude. Following the late Gustavo Gutiérrez, we must recognize the very biblical and theological foundations of the humanity of the poor as we participate in the grace of solidarity. Neoliberalism's spiritual dehumanization is an obstruction to the Reign of God that cooperative grace must overcome. When we recognize how spiritual dehumanization is dynamically at play with the

---

63. Martin Luther King Jr., "Letter from a Birmingham Jail," https://www.africa.upenn.edu/Articles_Gen/Letter_Birmingham.html.

other dehumanizations of neoliberalism, our prophetic critique culminates with an indictment of neoliberalism as integral dehumanization and marks it as the common evil.

What can be done? What must be done? Where is our hope?

Humanizing Praxis

Critique without a recommendation for praxis falls flat, leaving one wanting for what to do next. We cannot stop at critique. Without concrete movement to praxis, we risk a downward spiral of perceived powerlessness and despair. I do not want to worsen what I have argued is an integral dehumanization by adding another layer of impotent lament to an already overwhelming situation.

Part of our realistic task must recognize that neoliberalism has foundationally infected societies and cultures throughout the world. It is a dominating cultural force that has left indelible marks on and through the Global North's cultural matrix. As mentioned above, neoliberal categories have become part of our language and the way we perceive ourselves, for better or worse. Even as I write these pages, I am thinking about gauging how good of a writing day it is in words produced rather than the less tangible elements of the writing process that still contribute to the project in meaningful ways. Even as I try to resist because I know this mental framework is dehumanizing, I fall back into patterns that have been ingrained in me by my neoliberal cultural matrix. It would take a concerted societal effort to undo this kind of influence, which is, quite frankly, not realistic if we rely solely on human effort.

This does not mean that resistance is futile. We can push back against these cultural trends through strategic approaches to mitigate the dehumanizing effects of neoliberalism. We can resist only by answering the prophetic call to take God's hand in shared effort to transform a world of violent power all the way down to its roots. We, with God and one another, can root the world in the life-giving soils of justice and peace. We need cooperative grace.

Our resistance, however, cannot be one that matches power with power, blow with blow. That will only lead to a cycle of decline and to further violence, hatred, and dehumanization. There must be a better way because Jesus showed us a better way. The Law of the Cross, as articulated by Bernard Lonergan, formulates this better way in the following thesis:

> This is why the Son of God became man, suffered, died, and was raised again: because divine wisdom has ordained and divine goodness has willed, not to do away with the evils of the human race through power, but to convert those evils into a supreme good according to the just and mysterious Law of the Cross.[64]

The true power of Jesus of Nazareth is grounded in his powerlessness, which does not necessarily mean impotence. Jesus's powerlessness comes from the *choice* not to return violence with violence, power with power. Instead, the violence and power directed at Jesus is transformed into the miracle of the resurrection—a new life that is promised by way of God's love for each one of us. The enlivening transformation, accomplished by love and grace, must be the model for our resistance.

The Law of the Cross provides two key elements that we must model in our resistance to neoliberalism's dehumanizing effects: creativity and healing. Lonergan puts these two elements to work in a short essay entitled "Healing and Creating in History," in which he emphasizes how love is integral to the entire process:

---

64. Bernard Lonergan, "Part 5: Thesis 17," in *Collected Works of Bernard Lonergan, Vol. 9: The Redemption*, ed. Robert M. Doran, H. Daniel Monsour, and Jeremy D. Wilkins (Toronto: University of Toronto Press, 2018), 197.

> Where hatred reinforces bias, love dissolves it, whether it be the bias of unconscious motivation, the bias of individual or group egoism, or the bias of omnicompetent, short-sighted common sense. Where hatred plods around in ever narrower vicious circles, love breaks the bonds of psychological and social determinisms with the conviction of faith and the power of hope.[65]

Lonergan's point is that love conquers all forms of bias, which is a conceptual framework that harmonizes with the integral dehumanization discussed above.[66] While love builds a foundation for creating new values and practices that reflect these values, it can also heal the broken and failing structures and allow them to transform into something that can promote flourishing. The creating and healing vectors mirror one another and provide some level of hope even when things look darkest.

Most importantly, creating and healing love is attentive to the complexities of our world's beautiful diversity. As a theologian, I can do no more than offer mere sketches of what must be done to remove neoliberalism's obstructions to the Reign of God. Not only do I not have all of the practical knowledge and skills to dive into the particularities of effective and faithful practice in each context for humanization and flourishing, none of us does on our own. If we are to avoid the dangers of top-down abstraction by faithfully articulating and responding to the historicized, concrete evils in our world, we must humbly leave open questions to be answered by those with a

---

65. Bernard Lonergan, "Healing and Creating in History," in *Collected Works of Bernard Lonergan, Vol. 16: A Third Collection*, ed. Robert M. Doran and John D. Dadosky (Toronto: University of Toronto Press, 2017), 94–103.

66. While Lonergan's work has a clear influence on my own thinking by way of the work of Robert M. Doran, a full analysis of the Lonerganian influences on integral dehumanization is beyond the scope of this project and must be tabled for the time being.

level of expertise in their respective areas. From my perspective, the areas of humanizing praxis that provide the most support in removing neoliberalism's obstructions must promote and strengthen liberal arts education, economic policies that empower and protect rather than dehumanize, and a renewed commitment from the church to minister to the poor and the marginalized.

The Recentering of the Liberal Arts in Education

We must reconsider our educational systems and how neoliberalism has moved away from the liberal arts. The results of this shift in education from a liberal arts focus to a more "professional" focus can be seen in what Pope Francis refers to as the technocratic paradigm. In *Laudato si'*, Francis defines this paradigm in the following way:

> The basic problem goes even deeper: it is the way that humanity has taken up technology and its development *according to an undifferentiated and one-dimensional paradigm*. This paradigm exalts the concept of a subject who, using logical and rational procedures, progressively approaches and gains control over an external object. This subject makes every effort to establish the scientific and experimental method, which in itself is already a technique of possession, mastery and transformation.[67]

The technocratic paradigm is a key component of the neoliberal anthropology as it has been critiqued by Hinkelammert, Sung, Day, and others. While specialization at a certain level is important, making it the totalizing focus of one's education leads to the emphasis on domination that Francis critiques in his attention to the care for our common home that is central for a right

---

67. *Laudato si'*, §106.

relationship with creation. When applied to the question of education, especially at the high school and college levels, the technocratic paradigm focuses on test scores and one's viability on the job market as a sign of success.[68] Even as business schools and other preprofessional majors can provide important humanizing formation, they cannot be the totalizing focus of education.

Neoliberal truncation of intellect and education has insisted that we forget a fundamental truth about education: education is not merely about the passing on of technical knowledge or the development of skills; nor are these aspects of education the sole factors that make a candidate appealing on the job market. Again, these aspects can be good elements of an education, but they are not the end-all and be-all.

Education, at its core, is formation. Through the relationships with instructors, texts, fellow students, and one's own experiencing, learning self, a person changes. These changes, for better or worse, stay with us the rest of our lives. I can think of countless teachers and professors who fundamentally changed me during my studies, both as a high-school student and a university student. I read texts that rocked my worldview at its core and caused me to rethink things deeply. The relationships that I built during my years as a student have lasted decades in some cases. Each aspect has formed me as a person, and many people I know would say the same. The formation that we can experience through education can be as foundational as the formation that happens through one's family life, religious upbringing, and friendships.

---

68. This is also true of vocational programs; however their emphasis on education and formation is intended to take on a more professional form, putting them in a different category than that of the college preparation track of high schools and higher education.

The core of this formation happens through the study of the liberal arts and its emphasis on the holistic view of the human person. By studying the humanities and social sciences in a complementary manner, one's understanding of what it means to be human fundamentally shifts. We cannot view the human person as fundamentally only one thing or another, a wholly subsumed, yet cut-off from all relations and "sufficient" thing. The liberal arts force one to recognize human complexity. Learning the arts, history, literature, philosophy, and theology all together, one receives an education that encourages holistic growth, so long as one is open to it.

Neoliberalism's influence on colleges and universities in the last four-and-a-half decades is a fundamental challenge to educational models that prioritize holistic formation. Gerald Beyer, using the language of corporatized higher education, convincingly argues that this neoliberal shift is in tension with Catholic social teaching. In his analysis, the move in higher education to become more like a business, serving students as customers in the marketplace of universities, moves away from the liberal education that ought to be the core of the Catholic university. This shift includes a dehumanizing impact on poor prospective students. Beyer writes, "This capitalistic vision of education views education as an entitlement of those who can pay for it, and leaves students who cannot as fodder for the lending industry."[69] Beyer's analysis pinpoints the intersection of neoliberalism's social and intellectual dehumanizations. In places where all persons should be accepted in a community of learners, those without financial means are seen as second-class citizens. Rather than taking this approach, the humanizing answer

---

69. Gerald J. Beyer, *Just Universities: Catholic Social Teaching Confronts Corporatized Higher Education* (New York: Fordham University Press, 2021), 15–16.

would be to structure financial aid for students who need it in such a way that they can make their way through their education with a robust sense of belonging and welcome.[70] Loyola University Chicago's Arrupe College is an institutional example that moves in the right direction, with a two-year academic program that provides affordability without sacrificing the principal focuses of a Catholic liberal arts education.

From an educational standpoint, a solution to questions about the liberal arts in the contemporary university lies in the focus on and investment in core curricula. One cannot expect every student to have a passion for theology or history. Our societies still need nurses, accountants, and elementary school teachers. Through required classes in the humanities and social sciences, an institution can ensure that each student has an opportunity to grow and develop in holistic ways while still being able to have a major that fits with their interests and career pursuits. The critical thinking and writing skills that are developed in a liberal arts core curriculum enhance a student's ability to excel in their chosen course of study, giving them an edge in whatever they pursue after graduation. The greater perspective on the complexities of the human person and the world in which we live informs their technical knowledge, positioning someone to make well-informed decisions that require more than an understanding of how specifics of a field function.

An accountant who took the required ethics courses on their path to graduate from a Catholic liberal arts university should be less inclined to adhere to the competitive and antagonistic values of neoliberal business activities. During their work auditing the books of some business, they may notice inconsis-

---

70. I fully acknowledge that this can be very difficult for tuition-dependent institutions for whom every dollar counts. As I said above, this is merely a sketch. Many details, such as this problem, still need to be worked out but are beyond the scope of this project.

tencies that show evidence of immoral or even illegal activity, such as cheating clients of money with illegal fee structures and the like. A person who has been formed in the truncated education of technical knowledge that characterizes neoliberalism has no incentive to do anything but stay out of the business that is not their own or seek to exploit the immorality for their own personal gain. On the other hand, someone formed by their education in the liberal arts, including their properly informed conscience, would be inclined to take action, whether it be alerting the authorities or their manager to figure out what to do next. This could be seen as an ideal situation, but the impacts of a liberal arts education, if one is open to that formation, can bring about this kind of ethical decision-making that actively removes the neoliberalism's obstructions to God's Reign.

The holistic formation that a person can experience in a liberal arts education can also be directed at the curriculum itself. A significant weakness of these core curriculum classes is that they can be biased toward the Western canon, ignoring important voices from the Global South and reifying a paternalistic narrowness and social dehumanization. When education is focused on the praxis of integral humanization, however, this kind of problem becomes relatively easy to fix. Students, educators, and institutions should participate in the dynamic relationality of our complex world by adjusting the course readings and experiences to include often-ignored people, thereby heightening the critical consciousness of the social and political forces that shape our lives. This is also part of what makes the liberal arts education a unique and wonderful kind of formation: there is always more to learn and discover. If one is successfully formed by this kind of education, that desire to learn and discover takes hold and becomes an integral part of who that student is. This is a humanizing effect; it leads one to a kind of intellectual flourishing that cannot be easily replicated.

There are other great problems across higher education that do contribute to neoliberalism's integrally dehumanizing effects, and those problems span administrative issues that are beyond the scope of this project.[71] In addressing the matrices of problems, the emphasis must remain on the power of the liberal arts to humanize students and educators alike, which in turn encourages them to make choices that will humanize others.

Economic Policies that Empower and Protect

Establishing economic policies that humanize rather than dehumanize involves decisions and practices that fundamentally empower and protect persons and peoples in the political economy. Rooting our careful thought and analysis in practical concerns, we must move toward a humanizing economy that embodies the Reign of God. The humanizing framework emerges from neither a capitalist nor a socialist ideology. Following Ellacuría, I am critical of both positions because their historical manifestations still left the poor behind. Whether it be the communism of the Soviet Union or the neoliberal capitalism of the United States, the poor and marginalized are left beaten, broken, and damned to an existence of living in dehumanizing squalor. Both systems are broken, and their ideologizations only lead to the integral dehumanization described above. We must create a new way of practicing and thinking about economic policy that is, at its core, concerned

---

71. A particularly important issue that bears mentioning is the matter of justice for adjunct faculty, considering the significant number of core courses at liberal arts colleges and universities that are taught by them. These overworked and underpaid instructors are some students' only contact with the liberal arts. In their overextended state, these adjunct faculty may not be able to provide the same level of instruction as a tenure-track faculty member, depriving students of the liberal arts education and formation they deserve. For more on justice for adjunct faculty, see Beyer, *Just Universities*, 47–89.

with the well-being of human beings and preventing the erosion of their dignity.

First, economic policy must emphasize people over corporations and moneyed interests. A landmark event in this narrative is the 2010 U.S. Supreme Court decision *Citizens United*. Political theorist Wendy Brown has argued that Justice Anthony Kennedy's majority opinion is a clear example of neoliberal jurisprudence.[72] Kennedy's opinion explicitly transforms the *homo politicus* into the *homo oeconomicus* in American legal precedent by taking political concepts, such as citizenship and rights, and replacing them with economic analogues.[73]

The most significant way that Kennedy does this is by providing a neoliberal reading of the First Amendment to the U.S. Constitution. In his opinion, Kennedy articulates the idea of money as speech[74] in electoral politics in a new way: he claims that speech is like capital.[75] In short, speech, like capital, is a natural and good force "that can be wrongly impeded and encumbered, but never quashed" because speech, like capital, can proliferate and circulate.[76] For Kennedy, individuals and corporations are both producers and consumers of speech, which should not be regulated by the government under the

---

72. Wendy Brown, *Undoing the Demos* (New York: Zone Books, 2015), 154–55.
73. Brown, *Undoing the Demos*, 155.
74. This phrase is used as justification for individuals to make unlimited donations to candidates running for elected office by arguing that political donations are a method by which individuals can express their political opinions, which is protected by the First Amendment.
75. Brown, *Undoing the Demos*, 156.
76. Brown, *Undoing the Demos*, 159. Kennedy's language in the opinion is not as clear as Brown presents on this point, but if one looks to the location Brown cites, Kennedy uses the language of anti-regulation, which is a central neoliberal concept. For our purposes, Brown's argument, while imperfect, is sufficient.

protections of the First Amendment.⁷⁷ Brown draws connections between Kennedy's opinion and neoliberal economist Gary Becker's conception of the human person as primarily consumer, showing how deeply Kennedy's thought is steeped in neoliberal ideology. Brown argues that Kennedy goes a step further when he recognizes speech to be "innovative and productive, just as capital is."⁷⁸ Here, Kennedy replaces political, or perhaps even humanistic, categories with roughly parallel economic categories. A humanist might follow Brown and emphasize that the creativity of language has provided the conditions for the possibility of political discourse, philosophy, literature, poetry, and drama: a creativity that is good for its ability to connect the human race in communication and develop cultural achievements. A neoliberal economist, on the other hand, might follow Kennedy's opinion and emphasize speech as something that can be productive so long as it is not held back by government intervention.⁷⁹

Citizens United simultaneously anthropomorphizes corporations while dehumanizing people by drawing comparisons that allow corporations to appear to be similar to human beings, therefore requiring the same rights as human beings. This is dehumanizing by truncating the human being into nothing more than a *homo oeconomicus*, a "firm" operating in the market, ready for investment in order to compete with others in seeking particular goods or interests. Obviously, very few individuals could compete with the significant resources of corporations. It is simply not feasible. The law, then, must be used to contain and control these larger firms and ensure there is a just distribution of necessary goods and services. Rather than ensuring that businesses flourish with ever-growing profits, the

---

77. Brown, *Undoing the Demos*, 159.
78. Brown, *Undoing the Demos*, 159.
79. Brown, *Undoing the Demos*, 159–60.

government must see to the good of the populace, which is further dehumanized by the overwhelming competition.

Subsidizing childcare is an example of a concrete policy and practice that could make significant progress for both empowering and protecting people. Exorbitantly expensive, the average annual cost of childcare for infants is, in a lot of cases, like a second rent or mortgage payment.[80] Such an amount of money can be backbreaking for a lot of families. It is sometimes so much that one parent is required to leave the workforce, further lowering a family's total income. Tax credits can only do so much, as parents with young children are left vulnerable, overextended, and alone. When this pressure is added to the exhausting work of ensuring that small children stay safe and healthy, many parents can reach a breaking point, which leads to their psychological dehumanization.

If the government were to subsidize childcare at a 50 percent rate, that could add on average nearly $11,000 annually to a family's budget, which is a life-changing amount.[81] This would take a tremendous amount of stress off a family, especially considering how finance-related stressors can lead to psychological distress.[82] This is just one of many ways to address the psychological dehumanization caused by neoliberalism's hypercompetitive framework and emphasis on financial gain. There have been concrete proposals in the U.S. Senate, but, unfortunately, nothing has moved forward.[83] Such a step would, however, have

---

80. Economic Policy Institute, "Child Care Costs in the United States," https://www.epi.org/child-care-costs-in-the-united-states/#/DC (updated February 2025).
81. This number would be adjusted based on the location, but it would be still safe to say it is a life-changing amount of money.
82. Soomin Ryu and Lu Fan, "The Relationship between Financial Worries and Psychological Distress among U.S. Adults," *Journal of Family and Economic Issues* 44 (March 2023), 16–33.
83. "Warren, Sherrill, Lawmakers Unveil New Child Care Bill," Feb-

a humanizing effect on parents around the country who are seeking ways to keep their families afloat while ensuring their children are cared for while they are at work.

Financial support for nongovernment-run social services, such as food banks, soup kitchens, homeless shelters, and charity medical clinics, could further economic humanization. These direct services have major impacts on the lives of those who are struggling with food insecurity, poverty, and homelessness. While there are some resources in this regard, the $1.6 billon spent on various programs is miniscule in the face of the requested $842 billion for the Department of Defense for the fiscal year 2024.[84] Government spending on The Emergency Food Assistance Program equates to 0.19 percent of the defense budget. Even quadruple growth in spending on empowering and protecting people in their food security would barely scratch the surface of budgets for violent power. This kind of fiscal policy decision shows our cultural priorities by revealing and enacting our responsibility to the poor and marginalized.

Finally and briefly, we return to our earlier discussion of substantial access to the internet as a necessity in contemporary society. While costs can range from $20 to $300 per month, a great deal of the variation depends on location and internet speed. Subsidies through programs like the Affordable Connectivity Program can help address the raw monetary cost, but

---

ruary 8, 2023, https://www.warren.senate.gov/newsroom/press-releases/warren-sherrill-lawmakers-unveil-new-child-care-bill.

84. The U.S. government has The Emergency Food Assistance Program (TEFAP), which spent $1.6 billon on various food-related relief services, helping to fund various programs. See Congressional Research Services, *The Emergency Food Assistance Program (TEFAP): Background and Funding* (Washington, DC, 2023), 21; Chief Financial Officer of the Office of the Undersecretary of Defense, *Defense Budget Overview: United States Department of Defense Fiscal Year 2024 Budget Request* (Washington, DC: United States Department of Defense, 2023), 1–3.

they do not solve the issues of reliability of service or access to devices that allow one to accomplish one's necessary tasks.[85] In a society that is consistently moving into digital spaces, the poor and marginalized, the un-accessing and inaccessible, must become the preferential focus of our political economies.

The Church's Ministry

The institutional church cannot wash its hands of responsibilities in the midst of our neoliberal society. The gospel message is simple: minister to the poor and the marginalized because of, in, and through love. This message can no longer float in the ether as an abstract "common good." We must take concrete action in a humanizing praxis of the church.

Writing in the *Catholic Worker*, Dorothy Day challenged parishes: "Every parish should have its Works of Mercy Center, where the poor are fed daily, without question, in the name of Jesus Christ who Himself was hungry and homeless at times on this earth."[86] Day's call serves as the foundation for precisely understanding the church's humanizing mission and praxis. Feeding the hungry and sheltering the homeless are both explicitly stated corporal works of mercy, which means that it is part of the vocation of the universal church to practice these activities. While Day acknowledges concerns about the funds that are necessary to accomplish the work (noting that divine providence will provide), curating church finances and resource allocation in humanizing mission opens doors for potential creative solutions that enact the Reign of God.

---

85. Nick Cellucci and Timothy Moore, "How Much Does Internet Cost a Month?" *Forbes Home*, October 31, 2024, https://www.forbes.com/home-improvement/internet/internet-cost-per-month/#scrollto_6_ways_to_.

86. Dorothy Day, "Day after Day—More Houses of Hospitality," *Catholic Worker*, March 1, 1938.

Parishes are, first and foremost, about people. The community of a parish is essential to its overall health. If people simply go to church for an hour on Sundays and do not see their lives in the parish as an opportunity to come together in community beyond the confines of Mass, then the parish is not healthy. The most up-to-date buildings and the most efficient and affluent budgets can neither cover up nor pay their way out of the dis-eased parish. Buildings and budgets can, however, be tools for empowering, protecting, and fostering people as they grow into life-in-Christ together. Sometimes, it can be as simple as providing coffee and donuts in the parish center after Masses and giving members of the community a context in which to socialize and foster budding or lifelong friendships. It can also take the form of various ministries that bring the community together, such as youth and young adult ministries, ministries to homebound or ill members of the community, or countless other thematic ventures. It can also take the form of providing sanctuary to the refugee, health care to the sick, recovery to the addict, safety to the vulnerable, and education for every learner.

Many of these ministries already exist in parishes around the United States. The structures are already there, making humanizing praxis a matter of revitalization rather than building anew. Members of the parish community can bring their time and talent to the table to become a community of missionary disciples in these ministries. These kinds of ministries send a message to the wider community outside of the parish: we care about the people who come to us. If you are looking for a place to belong, we welcome you with open arms. This kind of attitude can make a significant difference in the way a parish operates and how the parish is viewed by the wider community. If the parish is seen as a missional place, where everyone is recognized as a sibling in Christ who is made in the image and likeness of God, those most in need of community will seek it out.

In the Catholic Church today, there is a significant need for LGBTQ+ ministries that genuinely welcome and love our siblings in that community. Following James Martin, S.J., and his tremendous work in LGBTQ+ ministry, Catholic parishes have both an opportunity and an obligation to be welcoming to members of the LGBTQ+ community, especially considering the way the community is continuously dehumanized. While there is a greater acceptance of diversity of human sexuality now than even ten years ago, there is still a significant, vocal part of the population that fears and hates people who deviate from the norms of heterosexuality and the gender binary. The community lives in constant fear of violence and death, with few genuinely safe places to go. In short, they experience an integral dehumanization unique to that lived experience.

Even the cultural acceptance of members of the LGBTQ+ community outside of the church is shallow at best and further dehumanizing at worst. In line with the neoliberal desire to commodify everything, Pride Month has become a performative exercise for companies of all kinds of industries. Rather than focusing on the joy that comes from accepting who one is, all kinds of products are changed for thirty days, adorned with rainbows no different than how items are adorned with hearts and Cupid's arrows for Valentine's Day. This "rainbow capitalism" does nothing to actually support the LGBTQ+ community, serving only to commodify this group and to further dehumanize them. There may be donations made to LGBTQ+ serving charities, but those donations become more about the tax breaks that kick in at a certain dollar amount. Members of this community, who have suffered an integral dehumanization in many cases, need and deserve more than rainbows printed on cans of Bud Light for a month.

The Catholic faith, however, can provide an alternative. With our call to recognize the inherent dignity of all human persons, there is a unique opportunity to welcome and humanize members of this community. We can recognize members of this community as our siblings, as fully human creatures with a dignity that no one can take away. While theologians wrestle with the questions about how this can square with Catholic doctrine on human sexuality, we can also take seriously Pope Francis's image of the church as a field hospital: there is a more important task at hand than strict doctrine. Our call is to first and foremost care for the needs of the marginalized, regardless of how well they fit into the picture of Catholic doctrine. If we are to follow the mission of Jesus, this must be the priority with all who are marginalized, even if it can be a challenge for us personally. As Copeland states, "Only an *ekklesia*, that follows Jesus of Nazareth in (re)marking its flesh as 'queer' as his own, may set a welcome table in the household of God."[87] There must be seats for everyone at the table, even those with whom we do not always see eye to eye.

This kind of care for the poor and marginalized must begin with a genuine love for the other. Following in Jesus's footsteps and continuing his mission as a community of missionary disciples are grounded in a life-giving, agapic love. This kind of love requires something from us and forces us to overcome our biases and preconceptions to be truly of service to and in ministry with those who need our love and hospitality the most. This love also requires us to be vulnerable to others to whom we may not normally open up. It can be uncomfortable, painfully so, to go beyond our bubbles to pull someone in from out of the cold. When we do, however, we participate in the cooperative grace that creates humanizing and salvific bonds for the person we help and for ourselves. We can be healed from our own dehumanizing attitudes. Cultivating personal relation-

---

87. M. Shawn Copeland, *Enfleshing Freedom: Body, Race, and Being*, 2nd ed. (Minneapolis, MN: Fortress Press, 2023), 69.

ships is the most significant act of humanizing praxis a person can perform.

Neoliberalism is the common evil. Using the work of various theologians as well as my own research, the injustice has been identified, the prophetic critique has been made, and three examples of humanizing praxis have been offered. May this sketch launch us into the work that must be done to reveal and enact the Reign of God. I pray that these pages have cleared a few steps of the path, so that you might further our journey together with your own research and praxis. Where the path will lead is undetermined, but we live into hope. Humanizing praxis can only happen in a spirit of love, as we are graced for the work together.

POSTLUDE

With Love Must Come Hope

> Our belief is often strongest when it should be weakest. That is the nature of hope.
>
> Brandon Sanderson,
> *Mistborn: The Final Empire*

While I have proposed several humanizing praxes as a starting point for resisting neoliberalism, it is worth asking a few questions about how we, as a church and a society, respond to the common evil, both in general and in the form of neoliberalism. What other theological considerations might we give to the common evil? Can the common evil, specifically neoliberalism, be overcome? Given all of these factors, where does the genuine hope we so desperately need come from? By addressing these questions in turn, we will have a fuller picture of where we must go from here.

Further Theological Considerations

Theologically considering the common evil, especially as integral dehumanization, evokes theological reflections on the life and dignity of the human person and the implications of the sanctity of life. The dignity of the human person is about more than just a heartbeat and the physical requirements of being alive. A central theme of Catholic social teaching, the dignity of the human person is about what allows a human being to flourish, living a life of significance with their integral needs met. The sanctity of life, then, must be about treasuring all of those things and ensuring the right of the entire human family to be able to flourish.

Cardinal Joseph Bernardin's consistent ethic of life calls our attention to recognize that human life is valuable and deserving of protection from conception to natural death. To heed his call seriously, we must heed the integral dehumanization of the common evil with its due seriousness. We accept that the inherent dignity of the human person, regardless of gender identity, race, sexual orientation, national origin, or any other descriptor, is immutable at all stages of life; this is a nonnegotiable of the Christian faith. To be consistent with that belief, we must vocally object to and actively resist anything that infringes on that dignity. One must, therefore, address instantiations of the common evil in neoliberalism, white supremacy, and xenophobic nationalism (to name but a few) as life issues, for they actively threaten the lives of the most vulnerable among us. We fail in our Christian vocation when we let these threats and harmful actions continue.

As we defend the sanctity of life in all ways that the common evil threatens it, we are called to see the face of Christ in those who have been victimized by the common evil. Engaging with the poor and marginalized from a position of privilege can take us out of our comfort zone; it can remind us of our own choices that may have exacerbated the conditions of "the least of these," condemn us for the times we looked away from their suffering, and force us to acknowledge our own privilege and what we have done or failed to do with the power it affords us. This vocation can be a very challenging aspect of our Christian life together continuing Jesus's saving work.

Seeing the face of Christ in the face of the dehumanized is further complicated by the social stigma associated with dehumanized groups, by the very social dehumanization that obstructs the Reign of God. The social dehumanization of addicts, the impoverished, immigrants, the disabled, racial minorities, and members of the LGBTQ+ community does not only affect the targeted community. The social pressures around us do not want us to be associated with these groups, socially dehumanizing each of us with lures of power and prestige or threats of our own infection by association. These social pressures, stemming from corrupted social, cultural, and religious values, impede and obstruct the relationships that fulfill our vocations as disciples of Christ, that reveal and enact the Reign of God in our midst.

Neoliberal ideologization, emphasizing that human value is determined by how and the degree to which one contributes to the economy, intensifies stigmas that have existed longer than neoliberalism itself. Neoliberal anthropology is particularly dangerous for those who are not major contributors to the economy or who cannot participate at all. A neoliberal worldview sees the working poor, the unhoused, the chronically infirm, the disabled, and others as leeches on society and, therefore, unworthy of our concern or help. This approach fundamentally opposes the way Jesus lived as described in the Gospels, where he intentionally spent his time with those on the margins instead of the powerful. He sought to bring comfort to those in suffering, regardless of their contribution to society or the economy.

The core problem is not a new one; it has likely been a stumbling block for Christians since the early church. Gustavo Gutiérrez's "A Hermeneutic of Hope" offers one of the most faithful responses to this common evil: "In the face of the poor, we must discover the face of Christ," and we must make this the fundamental decision of our Christian vocation.[1] Doing so

---

1. Gustavo Gutiérrez, "A Hermeneutic of Hope" (Vanderbilt University, 2012), https://as.vanderbilt.edu/clas-resources/media/A-Hermeneutic-of-Hope.pdf.

allows us to live in solidarity with and be of service to the people whom society has forgotten, even if our initial reactions and inclinations are not so Christ-like. This fundamental demand of Christian faith roots our humanizing praxis in the moments when the stigmas paralyze us. Seeing the face of Jesus in those who have been dehumanized allows us, to paraphrase Sobrino, to take them down from their crosses.

Overcoming Neoliberalism: A Realistic Possibility?

Overcoming neoliberalism is complicated. On the one hand, cultural, political, and economic systems have fallen throughout history, and neoliberalism is just such a system. Ursula K. Le Guin makes this concrete in her acceptance speech for the 2014 National Book Foundation Medal for Distinguished Contribution to American Letters: "We live in capitalism, its power seems inescapable—but then, so did the divine right of kings. Any human power can be resisted and changed by human beings."[2]

Neoliberalism's reign can end. It will require a conversion of many hearts and minds to heal religious, cultural, social, and vital values and establish a society that embodies a culture that prioritizes the flourishing of all human beings. The fall of neoliberalism is still possible through grace and the concerted effort of people of good will.

On the other hand, there is a particular insidiousness to neoliberalism that has allowed it to persist in one form or another for over four decades.[3] Cultural attitudes can take root within the hearts and minds of many groups that make up our society,

---

2. https://www.ursulakleguin.com/nbf-medal.
3. To see this at work from an economic policy perspective, see Jack Rasmus, *The Scourge of Neoliberalism: US Economic Policy from Reagan to Trump* (Atlanta, GA: Clarity Press, 2020). The cover image of the two titular presidents shaking hands at some point in the 1980s is rather striking as well.

and, while the formulation and presentation may change, the core principles do not. As we consider how neoliberal ideas have persisted through a changing cultural milieu, we begin to recognize how these ideas are not limited to explicit sociopolitical sources and theory. Popular culture is rife with the promotion of neoliberalism's values and dehumanizations as goods. There is a consistent line through film characters like *Wall Street*'s Gordon Gecko and *The Wolf of Wall Street*'s Jordan Belfort, even though the films were made twenty-five years apart. We still celebrate the entrepreneur and other titans of industry. Tentpole films are not alone here, as plenty of storytelling continues to make marks on the cultural imagination that support neoliberal values, however subtly. Competition—and making money off of it—is still the highest priority.[4] We all await the next megacontract that will inch over Shohei Ohtani's seven-hundred-million-dollar deal with the Dodgers, and we clamor for the entertainment of sports gambling on athletic contests between eighteen- and twenty-two-year-olds.

The rise of techno-oligarchy in the United States is the prime example (no pun intended). Tech billionaires such as Jeff Bezos, Elon Musk, and Mark Zuckerburg play a significant role in our society, given the ways that their tech companies—Amazon, X (formerly Twitter), and Meta—have become so integral to modern life. With this shift in focus, the manner of dehumanization shifts. They do not seek only our participation in the market and our money. They also seek our data, including our healthcare and biogenetic data. These data then allow advertisers to target an individual more precisely with the goal of convincing us to spend our money in a particular way that provides extra motivation.

As an avid player of trading-card games, I am often in need

---

4. A clear example that critiques neoliberalism is writer/director Boots Riley's 2018 film *Sorry to Bother You.*

of various accessories as well as packs of cards. When I scroll through my Facebook or Instagram feed, I am bombarded with ads for deck boxes, card sleeves, playmats, and subscription services that will send monthly boxes of random booster packs to my door. I am already inclined to purchase all of these things, which makes the advertising more effective. While my hobby, albeit an expensive one, is quite a benign example, it demonstrates how data targeting works and the cost efficiency that it prioritizes. The use of our data can be much more malicious than trading cards. A person struggling with body-image issues could be preyed upon by companies pushing diet and exercise scams, which use that person's insecurities to make easy money. Gambling websites are pushed toward people likely to partake in those activities. This can be extremely detrimental to people struggling with gambling addictions who, at least in part, can avoid physical casinos. When gambling is offered in the comfort of one's own home or mobile device, the temptation to relapse becomes that much more difficult to fight off. Once again, we see companies preying on people for the sake of gaining a customer and therefore profit, even if it comes at the cost of a person's well-being. The human person is truncated into a source of clicks and consumption. Neoliberalism lives on, even if in a different form. The common evil is thriving.

The question then becomes whether neoliberalism will ever fully go away. This is also an uncertainty. Many other harmful ideologizations, such as eugenics, persist, even though there is a general cultural consensus that such ideas are harmful. In this respect, neoliberalism may never go away.

There is, however, a distinction that must be made between an ideologization going away and an ideologization being overcome. As mentioned above, various ideologizations still exist, but they do not have the same cultural hold they once did. They have been overcome, and neoliberalism can follow the same path. Once again, overcoming neoliberalism will require a great deal of collective effort, blessed by grace, but it still has a very real possibility of occurring.

I would very much prefer to say that neoliberalism will collapse soon and that our salvation from this evil is at hand. That would, unfortunately, be a lie; it would be another false hope like the one discussed in the prelude. And we cannot afford that. False hope comes at too steep a price; the eventual disappointment leads only to despair. If we are to hope at all, it must be a genuine hope, born not out of some vague utopian promise for the future but arising through something concrete, viable, and absolutely true. That thing can only be love.

A Love That Produces Hope

How is love concrete? How can love overcome such dehumanizing forces? When we consider the Christian understanding of love as an outpouring of the self that is modeled after Jesus's love, it becomes clear that we can ground our hope only in love.

We can begin with a reflection on Romans 5:5, a short pericope with profound impact on our understanding of the relationship between love and hope. St. Paul writes:

> And hope does not disappoint us, because God's love has been poured into our hearts through the Holy Spirit which has been given to us.

According to St. Paul, the Holy Spirit has been gifted to human beings as a way for God's love to connect with us and to be ever present for us. This is a love in which hope can take root without fear of it being a false hope. It is a perfect love, a love without condition or reservation. This is a love that heals the sin of the world.

The natural next question is, What does this love look like? As one might expect, Jesus. The life and mission of Jesus as presented in the Gospels provide us with a blueprint of what a divine love articulated in a human life looks like. There are three primary ways in which the Gospel narrative provides us examples: Jesus's choice to spend time with the marginalized, his emphasis on justice for members of this group, and his overcoming of fear regarding his eventual death.

Jesus preached that his mission was "to bring good news to the poor" (Luke 4:18). The Gospel accounts tell us that Jesus chose to spend his time not with the powerful and wealthy but with the poor and vulnerable. This choice is representative of a divine, selfless love. There was always the possibility that Jesus could have chosen otherwise. He, too, had free will. Yet still he chose not power and glory but compassion and accompaniment. Jesus's ministry is a perfect example of, using another phrase of Sobrino, "love that produces hope." The love that Jesus embodied for those whom society had rejected and cast aside produced a hope that allowed for these individuals to persist, to continue to live knowing that they are loved and seen as valuable in love regardless of what economic markets said. If no one else did, at least this teacher from Galilee did. Such a fundamental human connection, one that humanizes the other, can do wonders for the human spirit.

Likewise, Jesus's forgiveness produces a hope that cannot be found elsewhere. In the moment of forgiveness, whether it be in the context of Jesus's actions in the Gospels or the priest's embodying Jesus in the sacrament of reconciliation, one is offered new life with boundless possibilities. A person is no longer shackled to their sins and has the opportunity to be the person they want to be; they are able to grow unimpeded and try once more to hit the mark. To hear the words "your sins are forgiven" or "you are forgiven" is to be liberated on a fundamental level, and such liberation is rooted in an unconditional love, producing a hope one can trust. This is particularly powerful for those who are stuck in a theological model of temporal retribution, where one is punished in their earthly life for their sins.[5] Forgiveness allows one to recognize that the injustices that they endure are not a punishment for past wrongs but are, rather, caused by the corrupt actions of and sinful systems built by others.

The constructive critique of injustice continues in Jesus's model of self-emptying love. His advocacy for justice for the marginalized communities he spent his time with was not an impotent passivity. The parables, the Sermon on the Plain, and many other examples throughout the Gospel narratives show that Jesus pushed those in power to reconsider their actions and live in service to the poor and marginalized. As the Gospels show quite clearly, the point of power, even divine power, is not to rule over those subject to your authority but to be of service to these groups. As Jesus says in the Gospel of Matthew, "So the last will be first, and the first will be last" (20:16). By using his power to help others, Jesus exercised his love in his actions. These actions of love inspired hope within these communities, as we see with the various people with whom Jesus interacted. His advocacy for the poor and marginalized is part and parcel of his ministry, as the realization of the Reign of God is not only about interactions with individuals but acting on a greater social level. This is one aspect of the mission of the church as well the "historical sacrament of salvation," to use Ellacuría's language. Through advocacy on a social level, another aspect of Jesus's mission is continued in our world.

The final element from Jesus's life that serves as a point of emulation for a love that produces hope is the way that Jesus overcame his fear on the Mount of Olives. When we look at the depiction of Jesus's prayer before his arrest in the Gospel of Luke,

---

5. This theological viewpoint is critiqued in the Book of Job, particularly the way it is argued for Eliphaz. For a full treatment of this topic, see Gustavo Gutiérrez, *On Job: God-Talk and the Suffering of the Innocent*, trans. Matthew J. O'Connell (Maryknoll, NY: Orbis Books, 1987).

the author depicts Jesus very clearly as feeling common human emotions: terror and fear. At this point, Jesus knows he is going to die, and it will be a painful, humiliating, and dehumanizing process. His humanity is fully on display: "In his anguish he prayed more earnestly, and his sweat became like drops of blood falling down on the ground" (22:44). Jesus, the Incarnation, a person of the Holy Trinity, expresses anguish and terror at what will be his torture and eventual death.

This human moment shows perhaps one of the greatest moments of love in the Christian story. Jesus knew what was coming; he may not have known the exact details, but the writing on the wall was clear. At this moment, a genuine choice was present: Jesus could stay or he could run. He chose to stay, and he made this choice out of love for all creation. The terrible narrative of Good Friday—and its culmination in the glory of Easter Sunday—could have never come to be had Jesus not chosen to remain in Jerusalem. Through an act of profound love, Jesus remained and awaited the arrest that would begin his passion.

Jesus's choice in this moment shows a perfect love; a genuine outpouring of oneself (literally) is on display. This love is our salvation. This love drove Jesus to live among and minister to the poor and marginalized; he called out for justice for these groups and died because of these actions. The love that empowered his ministry is central to realizing the Reign of God, a ministry that we are graced to continue. The perfect love that roots our perfect hope empowers our own ministry, expanding our hope from our own salvation to the salvation of all creation.

Ellacuría's own hope undergirded his prophetic mission in El Salvador by participating in the prophetic ministry of Christ:

> It is said that in cultures that have grown old there is no longer a place for propheticism and utopia, but only for pragmatism and selfishness, for the countable verification of results, for the scientific calculation of input and

output—or, at best, for institutionalizing, legalizing, and ritualizing the spirit that renews all things. Whether this situation is inevitable or not, there are nonetheless still places where hope is not simply the cynical adding up of infinitesimal calculations; they are places to hope and "to give hope" against all the dogmatic verdicts that shut the door on the future of the project and the struggle.[6]

Without his genuine hope rooted in love, Ellacuría would not have been able to follow in Óscar Romero's footsteps to care for and support the people of El Salvador during the Salvadoran Civil War. His participation in Jesus's saving work would not have been possible without hope, even as it led to his martyrdom in the middle of the night on November 16, 1989.

And so it must be with us. We bear witness to and in a world where evil manifests in countless dehumanizing practices, including illegal deportation, imprisonment without due process, demands for unquestioning loyalty, and corruption at nearly level of our political order. The world, as it stands now, appears hopeless. We cannot give in to despair. We must remember the moments in our lives touched by genuine love, and we must cultivate the hope that grows through that love. We can overcome this cultural malaise, you and I, but we can only do so in hope-filled love, restoring our friendship with God as the core of who we are as human beings. As we find ourselves and one another again in this friendship, true hope, justice, and liberation will bear fruit for the life of the world.

---

6. Ignacio Ellacuría, "Utopia and Propheticism from Latin America: A Concrete Essay in Historical Soteriology," in J. Matthew Ashley, Kevin F. Burke, S.J., and Rodolfo Cardenal, S.J., eds., *A Grammar of Justice: The Legacy of Ignacio Ellacuría* (Maryknoll, NY: Orbis Books, 2014), 9.

Index

abuse victims, 29
acquiring mode, 131–33
Affordable Connectivity Program, 160, 161
Afghanistan, invasion by U.S., xii
"All Lives Matter" ideologization, xviii, xx
Anselm, Saint, emphasis on human activity, 53, 54
antisemitism, 33
Arbery, Ahmaud, xx
Aristotle
    on humans as political creatures, 35
    idealistic vision of the *polis*, 14
Arrupe College (Loyola University Chicago), 154
Assmann, Hugo, on the idolatry of the market, 129, 130
authoritarian policies, and intellectual dehumanization, 36

BadgerCare Plus, 90
Baker-Fletcher, Karen, understanding of *eros*, 132
bank failures, 130
basic needs, 86, 96
    failure to meet, 84, 86–88, 105
    satisfaction of, 83, 95, 96, 98, 101, 102, 111–13; and freedom from domination, 96
Bernardin, Joseph, and the consistent ethic of life, 167
Beyer, Gerald, on neoliberal view of higher education, 144, 153
Black Lives Matter, xviii, xx
Brown, Michael, xx, 61
Brown, Wendy, on neoliberal jurisprudence, 157, 158
Burke, Kevin, S.J., on history and human action, 46, 47

capital, as basis of development, 84–86
capitalism
    East and West, 84, 85, 86, 108, 131n36
    neoliberal, 125, 131, 156
    questioning of, 98, 98–99n33
    as structural injustice, 23
Catholic social teaching, 1–12, 96n27, 125n13, 153, 167
censorship, and intellectual dehumanization, 35
childcare, subsidized, 159
church
    failure to reject neoliberalism, 145, 146, 147
    humanizing ministry in neoliberal society, 161

church (cont.)
  loving action of, 51, 52
  responsibility for poor and marginalized, 52, 53
  as sacrament of liberation, 52, 53
church members, active role in salvation, 52–54
church representatives, abuse of minors, 38
churches, and dehumanization of LGBTQ+ persons, 37, 37n50, 38
Citizens United (Supreme Court decision), 142, 157, 158
civilization
  of poverty and of work, 94–103
  of wealth and of capital, 84–94
Coblentz, Jessica, on depression as "unhomelikeness," 29
common evil
  as counterpoint to common good, 12, 13, 39
  el mal común in Ellacuría, xxi, 12, 21, 22, 24
  as integral dehumanization, xxi, xxii, 2, 24–39
  neoliberalism as, 121, 166. *See Chapter 4*
  politico-theological method for addressing, xxi, xxii
  as structural, 22, 57
  and theologies of the cross, 40
  See neoliberalism
common good
  in Catholic social tradition, 1–12
  definition of and critique in Ellacuría, 13–17, 19
  law and government role in, 14
  as universal pursuit, 4
community, and civilization of poverty, 99–102
compassion, of Jesus, 44, 44n4
compassionate action, 72–75
  and use of resources, 76, 77
concrete evil, 18, 150
Cone, James H.
  on lynching in Jim Crow era, 60, 61
  on white supremacy, 58–61
connectivity, xi, xii. *See also* internet access
contextualization, and universal principles, 20
Copeland, M. Shawn
  and Catholic intellectual tradition, xiv, xv
  on chattel slavery, 59
  on solidarity as discipleship through action, 70–79
  on suffering, 71, 72
  on welcoming the poor and marginalized, 164
culture
  and meaning-making, xvi, xvii
  and refinement, acquisition of, 8, 8n11

Daly, Robert, on sacrifice in the ancient world, 129
data acquisition, and targeting, 170, 171
Day, Dorothy, and humanizing mission of the church, 161
Day, Keri
  on being alive, 131, 132

critique of neoliberalism,
130–34
on the erotic as a force for life,
133, 134
death, neoliberal perspective, 127
dehumanization
of capitalism and communism, 84, 108, 113, 156
in Ellacuría, 22, 23, 234
and lack of access to digital technology, 65–68
of the poor and marginalized, 88–94
and reign of sin and the common evil, 58
See also integral dehumanization; intellectual dehumanization; physical dehumanization; psychological dehumanization; social dehumanization; spiritual dehumanization
Desire, Market, Religion (Sung), 125–30
developed nations, 85, 86
digital technologies, as reign of sin, 65–70
discernment, and action, 118, 119
displacement, 29
Doran, Robert M., S.J.
and Catholic intellectual tradition, xiv
and maldistribution of vital goods, 18
and scale of values, 9, 10, 11, 22
on social grace, 78, 79
and structure of the common good, 9
use of Lonergan, 9, 10

Ecclesia in America (John Paul II), 135, 136
economic crisis (2007–2008), xii
economic policies, humanizing, 156
economy, as social need, 5
education
and access to technology, 67
as formation, 152–55
and human development, 35
as structural good, 87, 88
See also liberal arts education
el mal común. See common evil
El Salvador, totalitarian government in, 14, 15
Ellacuría, Ignacio, S.J.
on capitalism, 23, 24
on civilization of poverty and of work, 94–103
and common evil, xxi, 2, 12–24
on common property, 99, 100, 101, 101n38, 102
critique of common good, 13–17, 19
critique of the civilization of wealth and capital, 84–94
on dehumanization, 22, 23
on earthly mission of Jesus, 42, 43
on economic and humanist materialism, 89–93
and historical evil, 18, 19
on historical sin, 17, 18, 19
on historical soteriology, 54, 55
and historicization, 15
human person in liberation theology, 82
on humanizing work, 96–99

Ellacuría, Ignacio, S.J. (*cont.*)
   and ideology, xvi, xvii
   liberative political theology of, xiv, xv
   on the mission of the church, 49, 50, 51, 52, 53
   on praxis and the common good, 15
   and preferential option for the poor, 20
   prophetic critique of, 117
   on society, 13, 14
   and suspicion of the state, 16
   on unemployment as an economic and theological problem, 103–8
   on working to realize the Reign of God, 82, 83
employment
   and access to technology, 67, 68
   as structural good, 87, 88
   See also unemployment
eros, loss of, 130, 133, 134
ethic of life, consistent, 167
ethics, and the common good, 2n1
evil
   and the civilization of wealth, 84–94
   overcoming through praxis, 19
   and problem of theodicy, xiii
   See also common evil

face of Christ, in the poor and marginalized, 168
feminicide, as reign of sin, 61–65
Floyd, George, xx, 61
forgiveness, 173, 174

Francis, Pope
   on church as field hospital, 164
   and discernment of injustice, 115
   on neoliberalism, 121
   on the technocratic paradigm, 151
Friedman, Milton
   concept of freedom, 123
   economic theory of, 121, 123
   on human interiority, 123, 124
   understanding of charity, 124, 125

Gaudium et spes, on the common good, 1–6, 11, 25
genocide, 33
Gerard, René, on scapegoating, 32, 33
globalization, 84n6, 89n13
government, corrupt, 14, 15, 16
grace
   collaborative, and solidarity, 78, 79
   social, 78, 79
Gray, Freddie, xx
Gutiérrez, Gustavo
   on developmentalism, 6n5
   on the face of Christ in the poor, 168
   on the humanity of the poor, 147

Hayek, Friedrich von, economic theory of, 121, 128, 137
health care, universal, 96n27
health insurance system, in U.S., 31

Hinkelammert, Franz
    critique of Friedman's neoliberalism, 122–25
    theology of life of, 125
historical necessity, 48, 49, 71
historical sin, 17, 24
historicization
    and the common good, 15
    of Ellacuría, xv, xix–xxi, 15
    and ideologization, xviii–xxi
    of Jesus, 43
homelessness, 139, 140
homo oeconomicus, 157, 158
hope
    lack of, xii, xiii
    and prophetic critique, 117, 118
    as social praxis, 130, 134
human agency, historical nature of, 46, 47
human choice, and formation of history, 47
human conditions, truly human/less than human, 7, 8
human needs
    categories of, 4, 5
    interconnectedness of, 10, 11
    See also basic needs; vital goods
human person(s)
    commodification of, 131
    in Ellacuría's theology, 82
    inherent dignity of all, 163, 164, 166
    See also people/persons
humanizing praxis 118–19

The Ideological Weapons of Death (Hinkelammert), 123

ideologization
    elements of, xviii
    of Ellacuría, xv, xvi–xviii
ideology, in Ellacuría, xvi, xvii
idolatry of the market, 129, 130
Ignatius of Loyola, and sin as obstruction to Reign of God, 56, 57
Incarnation, 118, 175
industrialization, and evil, 18, 19
integral dehumanization
    common evil as, xxi, xxii, 2, 24–39
    See also dehumanization
integral human development, in Paul VI, 1, 6
intellectual dehumanization, xxi, xxii, 34–36
    of neoliberalism, 143, 144
intellectual needs, 5, 9, 12
international commerce, inequality in, 16
internet access, 65, 66, 67, 160, 161
Islamophobia, 33

Jesus
    advocacy for justice for the marginalized, 174
    focus on the poor and marginalized, 173, 174
    overcoming fear of death, 175
    political mission of, 42–46

Jim Crow laws, 15, 33
John Paul II, Pope
    critique of neoliberalism, 135, 136
    on dignifying and humanizing effect of work, 97

justice and freedom, in a theology of dissent, 111

Kennedy, Anthony, neoliberal jurisprudence of, 157, 158
King, Martin Luther, Jr., on silence of clergymen in civil rights struggle, 146, 147
Kingdom of God, arrival of, 44. *See also* Reign of God

Laborem exercens (John Paul II), 63, 89, 97
language, and meaning-making, xvi
Laudato si' (Pope Francis), 101n38
  on the technocratic paradigm, 151
law and government, role in common good, 14
Law of the Cross (Lonergan), 149, 150
Le Guin, Ursula K.
  on naming things, 21, 22
  on resistance to unjust systems, 169
LGBTQ+ ministry, 163, 164
LGBTQ+ persons, dehumanization of, 37
liberal arts education, 35
  strengthening of, 151–56
literacy, technological, 68
Lonergan, Bernard
  on asking questions, 34
  and the Law of the Cross, 149, 150
  and scale of values, xiv, 9, 10
  understanding of the good, 9

love
  and the overcoming of dehumanization, 172–77
  as social praxis, 130, 134
lynching, 60
lynching tree, and crucifixion, 61

Maiese, Michelle, impact of neoliberalism on mental-health issues, 140, 141
malnutrition, and common evil, 21, 22
Marcel, Gabriel, on the problem of evil, xiii, xiv
Martin, James, S.J., LGBTQ+ ministry of, 163
Martin, Trayvon, xx, 61
Marxist thought, 108, 109, 129
material poverty, 7
materialism, humanist and economic, 89–93
McClain, Elijah, xx
McDade, Tony, 61
mental illness, untreated, 29, 30
meritocracy, and capitalism, 83
Miller, Vincent, on neoliberal focus on individuals, 141, 142, 143
miracles, as liberative signs for the poor, 44
misinformation, and intellectual dehumanization, 35, 36
mission of Jesus, 42–46, 174, 175
mission of the church, 49–53
Monbiot, George, on neoliberalism, xxii
moral poverty, 7

naming evil, 21

natural necessity, 48, 49
nature, common enjoyment of, 100, 101
necessity, natural and historical, 48, 49
 and suffering, 71, 72
neoliberalism, xxii, 121, 122
 as the common evil, 121, 166
 definition, 122
 as first philosophy, 136–39
 and humanizing praxis, 148–64
 influence in education, 153
 as integral dehumanization, 139–44
 and necessary sacrifice, 128, 129
 overcoming, 169–72
 in popular culture, 170
 prophetic critique of, 135–48
 theological tenets of, 126, 127
 theology of, 144, 145
 See also common evil
No Child Left Behind Act (2001), 143
North American Free Trade Agreement, 62, 63

original sin, 49, 49n10
 as historical necessity, 49
 in neoliberal perspective, 128, 134, 145
 and private ownership, 99, 100

parable(s), 44
 of Good Samaritan, 26, 27
parish, ministry in neoliberal society, 161, 162

Paul VI, Pope
 on the common good, 6, 7, 11
 and integral human development, 6, 7
people/persons
 emphasis on, in economic policies, 157
 as individual and social creatures, 3, 4
 reduction to material unit, 36, 37
 rights and responsibilities, in Catholic social teaching, 4n4
 See also human person(s)
physical dehumanization, 26–28
 economic structures causing, 28
physical needs, 4, 9, 12, 26
 deprivation in neoliberalism, 139
Pineda-Madrid, Nancy
 on feminicide in Ciudad Juárez, 61, 62, 63
 on soteriology of Anselm, 53, 54
Pinochet, Augusto, neoliberal policies of, 123
planning, for action, 75, 76
polis, idealistic vision of, 14
political theology of dissent, xxii, 108–13
 and discernment of injustice, 113, 115–17
 and humanizing praxis, 113, 118–19
 and overcoming dehumanizing poverty, 112, 113
 and prophetic critique, 113, 117–18

politicking, antidemocratic, and intellectual dehumanization, 36
poor
  church's responsibility for, 52, 53
  dehumanization of, 88–94
  See also poor and marginalized; preferential option for the poor
poor and marginalized
  in communist and neoliberal capitalist economies, 156, 160, 161
  as focus of love and praxis, 1, 17, 39, 146, 164, 167
  in ministry of Jesus, 174, 175
  as object of church's mission, 53, 163, 164
  See also poor
Popper, Karl, and the paradox of tolerance, 33, 33n45, 34
Populorum progressio (Paul VI), xiv, xxi, 6, 9
  and the common good, 25
poverty, situational and generational, 88, 88n12
power, abuse of, 8
praxis
  in Ellacuría, 15
  humanizing, 70–79
  and mission of Jesus and of the church, 52–55
  and overcoming evil, 19
preferential option for the poor, 20, 43, 44, 109, 136, 161
private ownership, 99, 100, 100nn36, 37; 101, 101n39
privatization, 100

property, common, 99–102
prophets, biblical, and critique of injustice, 43, 117
psychological dehumanization, 29–31
  health-care structures causing, 30, 31
  in neoliberalism, 140
psychological needs, 4, 5, 9, 12

quantitative easing, 130, 130n35

Rahner, Karl
  on love of God and neighbor, 57
  and seeking transcendence, 5
Reagan (presidential) administration, and neoliberalism, 121, 122
realized evil, 21
Reign of God
  obstructing, 56–70
  realization of: as mission of Jesus, 42; as mission of the church, 50, 51
reign of sin
  digital technologies as, 65–68
  feminicide as, 61–65
  impact on people, 75
  as obstruction to the Reign of God, 56–58, 69, 78, 79
  white supremacy as, 58–61
Religious Resistance to Neoliberalism (Day), 130–34
revolution
  to overcome the common evil, 109, 110
  in structural values, 106

rugged individualism, in U.S. culture, 3n3

sacrament, 50, 51
    of liberation, 49, 50, 52, 53
sacrifice
    in Christian tradition, 129, 129n30
    in neoliberalism, 128, 129
Salvadoran Civil War, xv
salvation, as historical necessity, 47, 48
Samour, Héctor, on historical evil, 18
scale of values
    corruption in, 22
    levels of, 9, 10, 11
    in Lonergan, xiv, 9, 10
    in *Populorum progressio*, 7
    and Robert M. Doran, S.J., 2, 9, 10, 11, 22
scapegoating, 32, 33
"See, Judge, Act," 113–15, 119
self-love, and moral poverty, 7
self-sufficiency, in U.S. culture, 3n3
September 11 attack, xii
sexism, 33
sinful social structures, 57, 58
slavery
    in ancient world, 14
    in U.S., 59, 60
Sobrino, Jon
    and crucified people of history, xxi, 52
    on dehumanization and globalization, 89n13, 91, 92
    on forms of salvation, 95
    on political mission of Jesus, 45
    on salvation for oppressor and oppressed, 71
    on understanding Jesus's ministry, 44
social dehumanization, 32–34
    of neoliberalism, 141
    structures underlying, 33
social needs, 5, 9, 12
social safety net, 104
social services, government support for, 160
social status, disregard for, and prophetic critique, 117
social stigma, and neoliberal ideologization, 167
Solicitudo rei socialis (John Paul II), and super-development, 22
solidarity
    and compassionate action, 72–75
    cost of, 77
    and discipleship through praxis, 70–79
    as response to suffering, 71
spiritual abuse, 37
spiritual dehumanization, 36–38
    of neoliberalism, 144, 145
Spiritual Exercises (Ignatius of Loyola), 56
    and prayerful discernment, 116
spiritual needs, 5, 12
    in Catholic tradition, 5
Standards, of Satan and Christ, 56
state
    role in feminicide in Ciudad Juarez, 64, 65
    suspicion of, in Ellacuría, 16

structural goods, 87, 88
suffering
 and the common evil, 21, 22
 by natural and historical necessity, 71, 72
suicide, among transgender youth, 30
Sung, Jung Mo
 critique of Franz von Hayek, 128
 critique of neoliberalism, 125–30
 on providing basic needs, 126
 on theology in economics, 126, 127

Taylor, Breonna, xx, 61
technology
 and elimination of death, 127
 and historical evil, 18
techno-oligarchy, rise of, 170, 171
Thatcher (UK) government, and neoliberalism, 122, 142
theologians, need to engage neoliberalism, 122, 130
theology of dissent. *See* political theology of dissent
Thomas Aquinas, on knowing God, 126
Tobin, Theresa, on spiritual violence, 37n49
transgender youth, and suicide, 30
Trump, Donald, Christian support for, 146

unemployment
 as dehumanizing, 106
 as economic and theological problem, 103–8
 as a sin of the world, 105, 106
 in Third World, 103, 103n41, 104, 105
unhoused people, 27, 28
university, role in combatting institutional sin, 110, 111
utopian ideal, in Ellacuría, 82, 83, 101, 102, 103, 107

victim substitution, 32, 33, 34
Vincent de Paul, Saint, charity of, 124, 125
vital goods, maldistribution of, 18, 76, 86, 87, 94. *See also* basic needs; human needs

welcoming sinners, and ministry of hospitality, 44
white supremacy, xviii, 33, 58–61
 as reign of sin, 58–61
 in social structure, 47, 58, 59
Woodsome, Kate, on U.S. health insurance system, 31
work
 dignifying and humanizing effect of, 96, 97, 98, 99, 111, 112
 subjective sense of, 97, 98
 See also employment; unemployment
workers, exploitation of, 8

xenophobia, 33

Zacchaeus, gospel story of, 44
Zubiri, Xavier, and *el pecado histórico*, 17